Prospect for Renewal

The Future of the Liberal Arts College

Earl J. McGrath, Editor

PROSPECT FOR RENEWAL

Jossey-Bass Inc., Publishers
San Francisco • Washington • London • 1972

PROSPECT FOR RENEWAL
The Future of the Liberal Arts College
Earl J. McGrath, Editor

Published in Great Britain by
Jossey-Bass, Inc., Publishers
St. George's House
44 Hatton Garden, London E.C.1

Library of Congress Catalogue Card Number LC 75-189040

International Standard Book Number ISBN 0-87589-132-2

Manufactured in the United States of America

JACKET DESIGN BY WILLI BAUM

FIRST EDITION

Code 7217

The Jossey-Bass
Series in Higher Education

A publication of

Monmouth College
RICHARD D. STINE, *President*

Preface

*H*igher education, more than any other area of intellectual endeavor, dramatizes the explosion of knowledge. Senior members of the profession can recall when many teachers and researchers in higher education could claim that they had read all the significant literature in the field. As in other more recent disciplines ontogeny has recapitulated phylogeny. What was once a broad, obscurely defined body of general knowledge related to the purposes and programs of colleges and universities has in a few years become a vast literature of highly specialized treatises, reports, documents, and raw data. Even those who now spend their entire professional lives in teaching and investigation in this new discipline find it impossible to keep abreast of developments except in a very limited sector.

The members of the academic community whose interests lie in other disciplines because of the very fragmented nature of modern learning find it impossible to keep up on the innovative ideas in the theory and practice of higher education. They have their own fields to till. Perhaps the chief obstacle to the solution of the problems in the colleges and universities today is the lack of a common body of knowledge among those who have policy-making responsibility. No one can reasonably expect scholars in such fields as physics, history, and philosophy to read the ever-growing literature in the history, philosophy, and economics and management of higher education. If, however, they are to bring informed judgment to bear on the crucial issues which now face the academic community, they must at least be familiar with the significant ideas and the proposals being expounded by knowledgeable persons. And the whole range of knowledge must be brought to bear on the organic whole of institutional life.

The series of lectures which make up *Prospect for Renewal* was designed to do just that. To exemplify how one liberal arts college can exert vigorous leadership in coming to grips with its own academic, fiscal, and administrative problems, President Richard Stine invited to the campus of Monmouth College speakers capable of presenting a critical distillation of contemporary thought on a most inclusive range of topics in higher education. The lectures were so organized and scheduled as to focus the thought of scholars in various branches of higher education on some of the major problems which the independent liberal arts colleges must solve. Although the solution of these problems is essential for the survival of some of even the oldest colleges, the emphasis in the following chapters is less on the mere preservation of these institutions than on the enrichment and enhancement of their educational programs. This focus was inspired by the conviction of those who organized the series that alterations of policy and practice must be based upon a clarification of objectives and a reexamination of currently accepted procedures. Tinkering with the machinery of higher education will now be less than productive; it will lead only to complete breakdown, as it has already done in some institutions.

Prospect for Renewal, therefore, has two major purposes. First, to identify and illuminate the major issues and problems with which the entire membership of the liberal arts college communities must deal in the immediate future. Second, to present the practical proposals of recognized leaders in their fields on ways and means to make college education more vital, more meaningful, and more effective than it now is in preparing young people to live in the swiftly changing world of today and tomorrow.

Those whose primary professional responsibilities require them to be conversant with the corpus of knowledge in higher education will find in *Prospect for Renewal* a rich compendium of current thought. Those whose specialized activities lie in other fields can gain rewarding insights into the issues which all members of the academic community must join in resolving if the liberal arts college is to survive and continue to make its traditionally noteworthy contribution to this society. In addition, virtually every issue and problem discussed by these authors in relation to the liberal arts college is inherent in the other units that make up higher education. The proposals the authors make for dealing with these problems likewise apply with equal force to all the various institutions in the system.

Philadelphi, Arizona
February 1972

EARL J. MCGRATH

Contents

Preface ix

Contributors xiii

1. Prologue to Renewal 1
Richard D. Stine

2. Social Change, Human Development, and Higher Education 13
Arthur W. Chickering

3. New Values and Faculty Response 30
Nevitt Sanford

4. The Name of the Game is the Student 50
Sally Whelan Cassidy

5. Alternative Pathways to Liberal Education 62
Morris T. Keeton

6. Technology Rewards Its Teachers 86
R. Stafford North

7. Learning Environments 99
Conrad Hilberry

8. Marketing and Higher Education: Perspectives for Planning 115
Harold Mendelsohn

9. Rescuing the Small College: A Bold Approach 127
Earl J. McGrath

Index 152

Contributors

SALLY WHELAN CASSIDY, *professor of sociology, Monteith College, Wayne State University*

ARTHUR W. CHICKERING, *vice-president for academic affairs, Empire State College, State University of New York at Saratoga Springs*

CONRAD HILBERRY, *professor of English, Kalamazoo College*

MORRIS T. KEETON, *academic vice-president and professor of philosophy and religion, Antioch College*

EARL J. MCGRATH, *director, Higher Education Center, Temple University*

HAROLD MENDELSOHN, *professor and chairman, Department of Mass Communications, School of Communication Arts, University of Denver*

R. STAFFORD NORTH, *dean of the college, Oklahoma Christian College*

NEVITT SANFORD, *scientific director, Wright Institute, Berkeley*

RICHARD D. STINE, *president, Monmouth College*

Contributors

Chapter *1*

Prologue to Renewal

Richard D. Stine

The pervasive theme of *Prospectus for Renewal* is a description of how the private liberal arts college should analyze itself, differentiate new perspectives, achieve new understandings, and act on new knowledge. The secondary theme relates to the mounting financial distress of all higher education, demonstrates the need to improve the productivity of educational institutions, and explores ways to reach that goal. These are mind-jogging topics. The sensibilities of some readers may be violated by these themes. Others will challenge various assumptions—for instance, some may feel that productivity and education are mutually exclusive considerations, no more appropriate as discussion-mates than humanitarianism and Adolph Hitler or sociability and Howard Hughes.

The brief statements which begin this chapter reflect

the perspective of the president of one liberal arts college (among well over a thousand such institutions) on some principal issues and options which these colleges should consider. The remainder of the chapter serves as prologue to the differing views presented in the other chapters.

The process of social evolution, both from prehistoric to present times and within societies, has brought us from a state of elementary survival to one in which the increase of people and material possessions has been the driving creative force. But the cutting edge of civilization is no longer energized by a quest for population and affluence. Its ethic is directed toward man's relationship with man and with his natural environment; its creativity is directed toward self-development and the realization of human potential; its method of actualization is problem setting and problem solving; and its principal vehicle is education.

Now that overkill and ecologic disaster are increasingly imminent and social injustice persists, the self-development of mankind within a responsible social context has become a central goal. Less urgent but no less real is the whole host of problems which confront men and women daily in the world of work and in their personal lives. However, as a group of problem solvers our society is still in a state of infancy. We are like kindergartners trying to spell *love* with the wrong blocks. Much of society has not yet developed enough maturity to know that neat and instant solutions derive only from wishful thinking. While contemporary students may exhibit more sophistication about social problems than did those who preceded them, they will not advance the art of problem solving unless they learn to describe problems fully, to improve their grasp of how institutions can be changed and human potential enlarged, and to dedicate themselves to the principle that driving creativity is a vital function of our society and the individuals who compose it. It must be the business of education to instill such awareness.

A student today, whether his vocational interests are

scientific or nonscientific, should be able to comprehend the relationship between the laws of nature, the values of our cultures, the state of advancement of science and technology, and the organization and practices of institutions and individuals. Effective problem solving requires full comprehension of these relationships. Besides understanding methodology, the student must learn to see himself as a productive and responsible member of society and be able to relate theory to practice. To support such self-development, our colleges must enable students to explore problems and investigate possible solutions in a rigorous way. Students must perceive how learning occurs and must learn how to learn and how to ask questions. They must acquire facility in diagnosing wishful and oversimplified thought. They must also disavow the simplistic and sometimes arrogant activism of late adolescence, the trend toward alienation and privatism, and the apathy and disengagement of adulthood. Moreover, they must develop a set of values which enables them to use intellectual and technological competence toward responsible and productive ends.

During the early part of this century classical liberal arts education provided a vehicle for teaching students how to learn in that it was directed toward continuity of development and the relationship of one piece of learning to another. Concomitant with the decline of classical education, most colleges have encouraged students to sample a potpourri of courses at the introductory level. Without sufficiently rigorous grounding in basic theory, without pursuing a problem to its difficult advanced parts, and with little experience in meaningful work and integration of theory and practice, the graduates of this system, far from being fully prepared to grapple with the problems of society, exhibit signs of intellectual flabbiness. Thus, to achieve competent problem solving, the educational experience through which this competence is gained, must be improved; rigor must be reincorporated in the contemporary approach to liberal arts.

The information and technology explosion is forcing

the college to recognize that it cannot educate a student for his whole career but only for his initial position. A college student today should specialize no more than is necessary to be placed in the job market or graduate school. He should concentrate otherwise on becoming a self-directed human being capable of moving through various work roles and life roles. Few institutions provide adequate opportunity for such a program of study. The contribution of higher education to society in recent decades has been far more advanced in intellectual and technological areas than in affective and value-based learning. This unhappy state of affairs is attributable largely to the emphasis which university-based faculty place on scholarly attainment, demonstrated through a specialty, and to the influence they exercise over faculties as a whole. Although liberal arts colleges began as institutions dedicated to developing harmonious personalities, most present college programs and the values which support them are substantially altered by the university model. Many colleges have retreated from the effort to integrate affective, value-based learning and cognitive learning in the student's total development, a situation to be regretted on several counts:

First, individual development involves a complex of interactions between personal, interpersonal, and intellectual competences. Inhibition of growth in any of these areas retards and may arrest growth as a whole.

Second, in contemporary society the most sought after individuals have developed the capacity to learn independently and exhibit characteristics of creativity—openness to experience, broad perspective and interest, flexible thought, awareness of identity, strong motivation to utilize talent, perseverance and patience, and ability to assume the risks and consequences of actions taken—characteristics largely associated with affective learning.

Third, our society, acting in its problem-setting–problem-solving role, will not usher in a golden age. As rapidly as men and women solve old problems or see them disappear through social evolution, they will come to think and operate in new and different ways, and these new ways of acting will spawn new problems. Creativity for a self-renewing society will demand an extraordinary level of personality integration from its leadership. The development of such leadership potential presents a significant challenge to the liberal arts college.

Fourth, each college should assist its students to develop self-regulative mechanisms so that love, trust, and respect for others rather than cynical attitudes become the prevailing mode in community life and help to pattern behavior in the broad community. Such development will not occur on campuses which are preoccupied with disciplinary professionalism.

Fifth, the small size of the typical liberal arts college is especially suited to the development of a sense of community and a sense of identity by the student. The college is suited also to effecting integration of educational, personal, and vocational identities, without which the student today is seriously disadvantaged.

By whoring after false gods, many liberal arts colleges have lost their distinctiveness, entered into losing competition with universities, vitiated their social utility, weakened their appeal to students, and sapped their academic and financial resources. The price which has been paid is high. Undoing the damage and renewing liberal arts colleges so that they may exert leadership in education for self-development and realization of human potential will be a complex task. The needed changes are primarily ones of attitude—the wishes, values, and commitments of faculty interacting with the desires and expectations of students, administrators, trustees, and the public.

Such renewal, however, no matter how salutary and timely it may be, will not rescue most liberal arts colleges from the financial distress endemic to all higher education. Part of this problem, which must be attacked, is the low productivity of educational institutions. Educational productivity must be defined, ways to change rates of productivity must be identified, and lines of action congruent with institutional goals and operational objectives must be determined.

The widely accepted standard of industrial productivity, physical output per man hour of paid work time, provides an inadequate model for determining educational productivity. In education the consumer-student is a partner in production. Since learning can be achieved only by the learner, the student is the producer of increments in learning. The other partners—principally the faculty but including the whole gamut of programs of instruction, supporting services, and physical environment—either support or inhibit the ability of the student to learn. Inasmuch as the costs of education are distributed among instructional and supporting services and physical plant, the productivity of each program within these categories can be determined to the extent it is possible to set operational objectives in student development and to assess the effect of each program on the achievement of desired outputs.

When a college achieves the goal of developing independent learners and self-renewing human beings, educational productivity is increased. The student who becomes an independent, self-renewing member of society is freed from continuing his education in a formal institution and from draining human and physical resources which could be put to better use. Since his formal education is directed toward reducing his dependence on academic staff, the faculty should be able to work with large numbers of students. Moreover, faculty would no longer need to impart information which students can acquire on their own and could concentrate instead on managing the student's development as a learner. Such a realignment of roles would permit higher faculty-student ratios than presently exist in all but a very few of our private liberal arts colleges. A college which espouses these objectives should seek to discover the optimum relationship between desired outputs and measurable inputs—human and physical resources and their associated costs in combination with the factor of time. Effective development of this relationship is central to the task of improving educational productivity.

The constant theme of this selective discourse on issues and options and of the chapters which follow is institutional self-development through the same process of differentiation and integration which individual development requires.

In Chapter Two Arthur Chickering provides a conceptual framework for consideration of the issues and opportunities of higher education. Analyzing the factors which accelerate change in social conditions and human existence, he describes the shift in priorities from a production-consumption society to a society based on self-expansion and self-development. He concludes that the changing requirements of society and perceptions of human development will require major shifts in the function and structure of colleges. While Chickering's observations can be applied to all higher education, the importance he attaches to integration of cognitive, affective, and value-based learning carries a special message for colleges which have abandoned this approach.

In the third chapter, Nevitt Sanford discusses the changing function of the faculty. He finds three patterns of faculty reaction to new student values—stand-pat, radical-accommodating, and eclectic–self-developing—and describes how these three types of faculty view their roles as professors and identify with reference groups, disciplines, and students. Sanford whose major concern is the improvement of teaching, asserts that the prevailing mode of academic culture inhibits effective teaching and evaluation. Faculties must achieve a change in consciousness in order to permit changes in academic structure.

In Chapter Four, Sally Cassidy focuses on interrelationships within the academic community that differ from those presented by Sanford. While both examine the state of tension and evaluate the interplay of attitudes and behavior within separate faculty and student cultures, Sanford's primary concern is faculty development, whereas Cassidy's emphasis is upon freeing the student to take charge of his own education. Cassidy advocates facilitating the student's perception of the purposes and modus operandi of the college and helping the student understand the importance of curiosity and the joys of discovery. She identifies six distinct student cultures and demonstrates how they relate to faculty and to the task of learning. Having stressed the importance of enabling the student to identify early in his career with a "meaningful" faculty member, she characterizes the orientation of three clusters of meaningful teachers. Although she observes that Socratic-type professors undertake a disproportionately large responsibility for working with students, she looks upon this mix of professors and this pattern of student-faculty relationships as desirable. Such a combination does seem appropriate for a college which is integrally tied to a state university and which must serve a wide range of students. However, a private liberal arts college should develop a more restricted goal congruent with the needs and expectations of a definable student subgroup.

Morris Keeton's principal objective is to offer guidelines on how to design effective liberal arts programs. Drawing on the contracted studies program of Evergreen State College, the plan designed by David Bakan,[1] and the project-oriented studies program at Antioch, Keeton derives eleven guidelines which he qualifies as "examples" of relevant principles. One of these is the cardinal principle that increased motivation is likely to support learning. He states that motivation can be enhanced either through learning which involves significant ethical considerations or through work on problems of social priority. Another aid to learning is agreement of faculty and students on both expectations and objectives.

Keeton also asserts a need on the part of the student for

[1] "A Plan for a College," *Canadian University and College,* June 1969, 30–34, 42–43.

models of competence. He advocates freedom for the teacher to determine what and how he teaches and freedom for both students and faculty from restraints of the mechanical features of institutional policy. Keeton, however, stipulates that freedom must be exercised within the parameters of institutional goals and the programs that support these goals. His consistent theme is that the attitudes, practices, and structures in liberal education must be compatible and support each other.

While Keeton focuses on the relationship between programs and people in formulating guidelines, Stafford North elaborates a systems approach to educational planning. North has been intimately involved in developing a multimedia learning center at a college which uses both the system and the tools of instructional technology on an extensive basis. The system is based on designing operational objectives or desired outputs for students. Alternate means of achieving these objectives, including the tools of technology, must also be formulated. Continuing measurement and appraisal of the student and monitoring of his individual program are required from outset to completion, with needed adaptations along the way. North makes a strong case for use of instructional technology by liberal arts colleges on the basis that it frees teachers to devote more time to the more personal and human aspects of programs, to improve productivity, and to show accountability. However, the program he describes does not demonstrate a level of involvement of students in the planning of programs which would be consistent with their growth as independent learners.

In the succeeding chapter Conrad Hilberry concurs with North's argument that colleges must adopt the systems approach of instructional technology but suggests that information subject to programing be incorporated into small learning modules. For the remainder of the curriculum, Hilberry favors involvement of students and faculty in collaborative investigation of problems that interest and confound them both. He analyzes various learning environments and discusses factors which have reduced student identification with the traditional campus: student desire for experiences away from school (an impulse accentuated by sterile physical plants) and desire for intense personal relationships and social experimentation. To achieve cohesion in the learning environment, Hilberry insists that colleges make it easy for students to enroll and disenroll. He also advocates changes in the physical environment to establish a creative and pleasant atmosphere in which to live and work. Colleges which draw the boundaries of their learning environments around the classroom on the campus will not succeed in helping students to become doers as well as knowers.

Such varied components as attitudes and motivation, cultures and environment, systems and structures, and interaction of faculty and students influence the marketability and the marketing of an institution. As a researcher in social relations, attitudes and public opinion, marketing, and communications, Harold Mendelsohn applies these fields to the issues of marketability and marketing of colleges. He documents the increasingly accepted belief that the share of the market for private colleges is shrinking and that this trend will continue in the face of rising tuitions. He asserts that students will be increasingly attracted to colleges which can fashion a distinct identity to fill the needs of a student subgroup and which market their uniqueness effectively. To facilitate differentiation among institutions of higher education, Mendelsohn proposes a major research project to assemble information on social trends, develop typologies of future students, and create an understanding of the dynamics of marketing applied to an academic institution. He concludes that a healthy academic marketplace will prevail if government takes action to redeploy revenues among students so that they can choose whatever institution they wish.

The central message of Earl McGrath in the final chapter is that traditional means to raise income and control costs are insufficient and that many colleges will die unless they can increase educational productivity by decreasing the unit cost of instruction. He calls for a year's moratorium on added expense, during which a committee composed of all groups of the college, including trustees and alumni, would renew goals, set operational objectives, order priorities, and budget in conformity to policy decisions. Part of this management-by-objectives approach should involve a detailed analysis of management methods and practices to ensure that roles are clearly defined and long-term implications of resource allocations are clearly understood. In McGrath's concluding paragraph he states the principal vehicles for the survival and flourishing of the liberal arts colleges: "Wisdom in planning, boldness in execution, and unswerving commitment." Thus on renewal of academic management as well as academic programs, McGrath and other authors place the highest priority on changes in attitudes.

This book contains a substantial body of new information relevant to the problems of liberal arts colleges. It provides new insights, exhibits understanding of the dynamics of these problems, and suggests specific ways in which these insights can be utilized. However, many basic concepts of renewal have been expressed for a number of years by these authors. For instance, the messages of McGrath's *Memo to a College Faculty Member* (1961), Chickering's *Education and Identity* (1969), and Sanford's *Where Colleges Fail* (1969) were clearly communicated but have been largely ignored. In *Prospectus for Renewal* several of the authors demonstrate that the principal function of overall renewal is a change of attitude and consciousness. If such change occurs within academic communities, many solutions proposed in this book will become feasible.

A message from the quill of fra Giovanni, dated 1513, seems relevant to the problems of the colleges today and to the communications gap between advocates and potential agents of renewal:

The gloom of the world is but a shadow.
Behind it, yet within reach, is joy.
There is a radiance and a glory in the darkness,
Could we but see, and to see we have only to look.
I beseech you to look.

Gloomy withdrawal and paralysis of action are unthinkable responses to the problems and opportunities arising in our changing society and individual lives. Educators, instead, encouraged and supported by government, industry, and the citizenry as a whole, must become seekers of renewal. If academe becomes self-renewing, excitement and joy will be restored and education will provide an appropriate vehicle for the future growth of societies and men.

Chapter 2

Social Change, Human Development, and Higher Education

Arthur W. Chickering

"Alterations as usual while business is in progress"—that's the sign hanging on every major institution in the country. Higher education is no exception. Until recently, however, it was "business as usual": colleges and universities, like graveyards and mountains, were impervious to outside forces, impossible to change. But now, just as graveyards yield to thruways and mountains surrender to bulldozers, institutions of higher education are beginning to move in response to strong social forces. Although some hard-pressed institutions face the fundamental "To be or not to be?" question, most can still weather their troubled seas by asking, "What must I become?" Effective answers require sound judgments concerning social change and human development.

Social Change

Change tumbles us along. Fundamental changes in energy and work, in population and human contact, in generating information, and in the exchange of knowledge and experience create fundamental changes in human existence and human requirements. Half the energy consumed by man during the last two thousand years has been consumed during the last one hundred. In 1850 in the United States, 440 hours of horsepower were produced per person; in 1900 the figure was 1,030; in 1950 it was 4,470; and by 1958 it was more than 5,000. That's a lot of horses. But now the horses are different, and sources of energy have shifted. In 1850, people and animals produced 65 per cent of the horsepower; and inanimate sources 35 per cent, in 1950, 98 per cent was supplied by inanimate sources. Now people manage energy, in massive amounts. The work of the twentieth century—its satisfactions, its consequences, its implications—little resembles the work of the nineteenth. Human contact has become intense and inescapable. From the birth of Christ to the Civil War the world population grew from 300 million to one billion. At the end of the next one hundred years the latter figure had tripled. The average density of Colonial America was one person per square mile; human contact was circumscribed and a matter of choice. Now Chicago has more than three million in roughly the same area—a density of ten thousand persons per square mile—and there is no escape.

Like the population, information and the capacity to manipulate it also are expanding exponentially. One hundred thousand journals are published in more than sixty languages.

In 1956, fewer than one thousand computers were at work in the United States. Their capability was twelve billion computations per hour. This has increased to twenty trillion, and the typical machine is ten times smaller, one hundred times faster, one thousand times less expensive. Information exchange is almost immediate. Events in Chicago and Saigon are reexperienced the same day in Boston and Brussels; practices in Johannesburg affect policies in London.

Extensive information, rapid processing and exchange, intense and inescapable human contact, and massive energy to power the whole are the basic conditions for profound and accelerating change in social conditions and human existence. The consequence of these changes is a fundamental shift in the core of human existence. A new center of gravity is replacing that organizing force which has driven man since he crawled from the sea or was banished from Eden. Until the late twentieth century, most men—in all cultures and in all nations—spent most of their waking hours pursuing food, clothing, shelter, and physical safety. As man became more skilled in mastering his environment, as social organizations grew, and as agricultural practices were improved, basic needs were more readily obtained; man worked not simply for survival but for increasing comfort. This work has been highly successful. In the United States most persons have more than adequate food, clothing, and shelter; most live quite comfortably and securely. Furthermore, for more and more of us, simple comfort has given way to the desire for luxury.

In the last fifty to one hundred years our working life span has more than doubled. For many people retirement at sixty-five is premature and frustrating; sometimes it is the occasion for a new career. But many of us, by the time we're forty, or even thirty, have at least adequate incomes, insurance, and possessions. What purpose then is left for the next twenty, thirty, or forty years, for the second half of our working life span? What existential root will supply a satisfying existence?

We stave off boredom by turning toward sensuality. Fancy eating with good wines, becomes important. Sexual relationships become more flexible and free so we can frankly devote greater time, energy, and resources to such pursuits. Drugs open a new world in which many hours can be passed. But the problem is that the senses get satiated. They give transitory relief, but no lasting answers.

To be sure, large minorities in the United States, Canada, Japan, and Europe still lack basic necessities and simple comforts. It is also true that most of the rest of the world population lives in poverty and is consistently close to starvation. When that fact is put in the context of an expanding population in a finite space with finite resources, the other major force relocating our center of gravity becomes apparent. Before long the world must not only achieve a stable population, but also it must stabilize material production at a level consistent with the requirements of a closed ecological system with limited resources. Zero or near zero growth in gross national product, most of which ultimately becomes gross national garbage, must accompany zero population growth. Because the United States, with 6 per cent of the world's population, accounts for 40 per cent of the world's consumption, this country must develop the new center of gravity and by so doing help the rest of the world satisfy basic needs but avoid our own excesses.

The new center of gravity, the new motor for human existence, is self-expansion and self-development. We cannot ignore considerations of food, clothing, and comfort, but new priorities can move us toward a richer and more satisfying existence. We also make a fundamental social contribution, because the best thing we can do for other individuals and for society in general is to become more sensitive, competent, and effective. Furthermore, when the quality of our life and the potential for our own development are given first priority, the role and value of material possession shifts. When institutional priorities follow suit—as they are beginning to—we will begin to recognize new worlds of human potential.

Human Development

A successful and satisfying existence requires three kinds of competence: intellectual competence, professional or vocational ability, and interpersonal competence. Intellectual competence requires more than the capacity to memorize and assimilate information. It also requires the capacity to analyze concrete situations and experiences, as well as written materials, oral communications, mathematical symbols, and artistically presented realities; the capacity to synthesize materials from diverse sources; the capacity to weigh evidence and to distinguish the balance between fact and emotion. Professional and vocational abilities may or may not depend heavily upon general intellectual competence, but they are required for self-support and for social contribution and offer satisfactions in their own right. Job success and a satisfying life depend primarily, however, upon interpersonal competence. Almost all work and social situations call for the capacity to work effectively with other people, to understand what they're doing and why they're doing it, and to help them understand what you want them to do in such a way that they will do it.

Effective performance does not depend simply upon level of competence. It is powerfully influenced by sense of competence, by the self-confidence brought to a task. Every athlete—basketball player, baseball player, bowler, golfer, tennis player—knows how much self-confidence affects his performance. The same is true for a job and for life in general.

Competence is seldom pursued vigorously and effectively, however, unless it is guided by at least tentative commitment to some reasonably clear purposes. Clear purposes require decisions concerning vocational plans and aspirations, which in turn require judgments concerning life style. The kind of work pursued influences not only income but whether one lives in the country, a suburb, or a city, whether work is left at the office or must be taken home. It influences how much time and energy there is for spouse and children and for recreation. Choice of work influences the kinds of persons who become friends, the organizations joined, and, as time goes on, the values developed. When there is sufficient clarity to develop plans and to identify the steps required for their completion, energy can be turned more fully and efficiently to developing the competence to move ahead. A sense of our own competence is also essential, especially as a cornerstone for autonomy. Autonomy is different from independence. Independence means not subject to control by others, not requiring or relying on something else. When a man could raise his own food, hunt his own meat, make his own clothes, and build his own shelter, if he was competent, he could be independent. Now, however, we all must rely on others. We are all, therefore, not independent but interdependent. Our lives are, and increasingly will be, significantly affected by what happens in Russia, Southeast Asia, Africa, and Latin America as well as by what happens next door and around the corner. In a traffic jam, in an elevator when a blackout hits, in an airplane when the engine quits, we can be much more competent than everyone else, but there's not much we can do but sit and wait for someone else to take effective action.

Autonomy means having the capacity to be self-governing and having the right to do so. Each of us has the right and can develop the power to exercise our autonomy. We develop that power by managing our interdependence, by recognizing when and where we must depend on others and when we need not. By so doing we carve our own unique lives out of the historical, social, and individual conditions of our existence.

Life continually reveals us to ourselves, if we'll watch. And social changes frequently evoke self-examination: why did we act that way; where did those attitudes come from; why can't we cope with this task or that person? To answer such questions we become more attuned to our reactions; we search our backgrounds for clues. We try out new behaviors and test ourselves in new situations to see how we react and what we can learn. As times goes on we know ourselves more fully and richly. We develop a more realistic sense of both our limitations and our potentials.

Competence and autonomy, depend heavily upon understanding others, for it is primarily through relationships with others that competence, purposes, and autonomy develop. But understanding others is significant in itself. Our lives are enriched as we learn to enjoy a wider range of different kinds of persons; when we can go beyond simply putting up with those who are different and become able to respond to them as individuals rather than as members of a general class or category. Understanding is essential for lasting and intimate friendships; if they are to survive differences and periods of separation, they must rest on the mutual respect and trust which come from fundamental understanding.

Finally, there is the integrity that exists when word and deed are consistent with one another, when they represent a reasonably coherent set of beliefs and principles which do not become self-contradictory with changing circumstances and conditions. Developing integrity is a continuing two-part cycle. On the one hand, there is a constant effort to clarify what we believe and what we think, to establish a set of beliefs which make sense to us in terms of our own experiences and insights. On the other hand, there is the struggle to make our actions consistent with our beliefs, to act on our principles. Because life brings experiences which challenge our beliefs and which tempt or pressure us toward behaviors inconsistent with them, developing and maintaining integrity is a life long task.

These then are six major areas of development which everyone pursues in varying degrees throughout life: developing competence; clarifying purposes; becoming autonomous; understanding ourselves; understanding others; developing integrity. Challenge and response is a process fundamental to learning and development. Self-expansion and self-development occur as new conditions require new responses, as new experiences excite new reactions. To respond effectively we have to obtain additional information, acquire new skills, develop new sensitivities. Often we have to break longstanding habits and develop new ones—new ways of seeing ourselves and thinking about our possibilities, special skills, or different attitudes.

Whether or not challenge exists and whether or not learning occurs depends upon the characteristics of the person and the requirements of the situation. Sometimes the challenges are overwhelming. We can be damaged and can damage others in our misjudgment or frustration. Sometimes challenges are so easily managed that no learning or development occurs. The problem is to find the optimal distance between where we are and where new experiences can take us, so we can move ahead without too much risk to ourselves and others. Reflection must be followed by action. Only when we have put ourselves into new situations can development occur. When we move into challenging situations we also move into risk and uncertainty. But a living being without some areas of tension and growth is a vegetable. A satisfying experience continually balances the risks of the new against the safety of the old and maintains sufficient challenge that learning and development occur.

When the center of gravity shifts from the production and acquisition of material goods to personal expansion and development, major reorientations occur toward work, marriage and family living, friends and acquaintances, community participation, and education. We choose a job for the areas of competence it will foster, the different individuals to be worked with, the ideas it will provoke, the values it will question. Marriage and the family must support and strengthen individual differences in talents, sensitivities, interests, and desires—maintaining diverse styles to enhance the range of experience for all. Similarly, we open relationships with persons who differ, giving ourselves time to move beyond our stereotypes and to realize the satisfactions of diversity. Each of these areas needs substantial examination, but perhaps the implications are most powerful and most immediate for education.

Implications for Education

During the late 1960s the United States spent substantially more for education than for any other single activity, including defense. Between seventy and seventy-five billion dollars were invested annually, of which fifty billion was spent by public and private schools and universities, and twenty-five billion by industry, governments, and the armed forces for all kinds of schooling and training. These expenditures were twice those of the fifties and four times those of the years immediately after World War II. More is now spent on education than on all other nondefense services combined, and teachers are the largest occupational group in the country. Education has replaced birth, wealth, and talent as the key to opportunity and personal advancement, and it will become even more important in the future. The most important ingredient for a rapidly changing society are persons who have learned how to learn, who can pursue effectively their own development in response to shifting personal interests and social requirements. Reductions in defense and space expenditures have put thousands of physicists and engineers out of work. Effective retraining will depend primarily on their readiness and ability to assimilate new knowledge, grasp new concepts, and acquire new skills. The future will bring many similar dislocations. Society's capacity to cope will depend on the capacities of its educational institutions.

For the last hundred years the United States has made a little education universally available and a lot of education accessible to many. The time is coming when a lot of education will be universal, but its forms, its practices, and its relationship to an individual's total existence will be quite different. These new forms and practices already are emerging both in the United States and Great Britain. Generally, they recognize four major principles: education must become effectively integrated with the individual's total experience; the most effective learning occurs in the pursuit of significant personal plans and aspirations; sound learning and development require both direct and vicarious experiences, both action and reflection; and individual requirements will vary in timing, intensity, and substance, and in the balances between direct action and reflection.

Two major forces underlie the shift toward integration of educational activities with the rest of life. The first is what Peter Drucker calls the "knowledge economy." In 1900 the largest single group, and the majority of the American people, made a living on the farm. By 1940 the man on the assembly line, the industrial worker, the semiskilled machine operator dominated the work force. Today the center of the work force is the "knowledge worker," the person who applies ideas, concepts, and information to his job rather than manual skill or muscle.

Until the last half of this century, the boundaries between work and school were quite clear. You stopped going to school and went to work. That was the end of schooling. It certainly was not the end of learning, but it was the end of systematic and formal attempts to acquire new information, concepts, and abilities. Now, as knowledge becomes increasingly important to effective work, easy access to those educational activities pertinent to shifting individual requirements also becomes necessary.

Easy access means that timing and intensity must become much more flexible. In the past the pressure for increased knowledge and intellectual competence has been met by extending the years of schooling. This response still assumes the separation of schooling and work and that, in a given number of years, an individual can receive an education that will serve for the rest of his life. Even if those assumptions made sense a hundred years ago, which is doubtful, they are absurd now. None of us can foresee very clearly the knowledge and competence he will need ten or fifteen years from now. We do know that much of that knowledge does not yet exist. We know also that learning occurs most effectively when it connects with our immediate experiences and responsibilities and that learning is lost quickly if it is not built in through action and use.

The second major force moving us toward continuing education stems from the effect of learning itself. The more we know the more conscious we become of our own ignorance; the more we have learned the more we recognize the pertinence of additional education; the more diverse our competence, sensitivities, and sources of satisfaction, the more we are attuned to opportunities for growth and the readier we are to capitalize on them. Therefore, increased personal expansion and development set in motion a self-amplifying dynamic which extends the relationship between learning and life well beyond the vocational and professional demands of the knowledge economy.

These two concurrent and accelerating forces will lead to a new life style which moves dramatically away from its typical "all then nothing" approach to education. Education will be pursued intermittently for varying lengths of time and with varying degrees of intensity. During any given five-year period an individual will move in and out of relationships with an educational institution. He or she may work full-time in a residential setting for several months, or part-time independently or with a few persons with similar purposes in his home community. His educational program may intersperse brief residential periods of intensive study and exchange with others —long weekends, a week or two—with individual experience, writing, and reflection at home.

Continuing education will not be limited to specialized subjects pertinent to occupational requirements. It will include subjects of more general educational value—philosophy; history; literature; behavioral, social, and natural sciences. For the natural progression is not typically from generalist to specialist; more often the generalist is a specialist who relates his talents to general issues and recognizes the diverse areas of knowledge pertinent to his speciality. These reciprocal relationships continually increase the breadth of knowledge and awareness so that the links between different areas become even more apparent.

One consequence of the shift toward continuing education will be careful analysis of when various kinds of learning are best pursued. The study of philosophy, religion, and human development may be best pursued when major developmental transitions are underway: during late adolescence and young adulthood, again during the forties when children have left home and new careers may be anticipated, and again upon retirement, with each subsequent period enriched by a larger pool of wisdom and experience. Managerial and professional learning in business, law, medicine, engineering, education, architecture, and many other areas may be the focus of effort during the most active and productive years from twenty-five to forty or fifty. In such areas the young person cannot learn all he needs to know before he starts and the advanced practitioner needs new information and increased competence.

As educational activities become integrated with the rest of life the center of attention will shift from institutions to individuals. As more people take the initiative for their continued learning and development, their varying needs and purposes will become the point of departure for curriculum, teaching, and evaluation. Preplanned and prepackaged courses, television series, programed learning materials, computer assisted instruction, and other instructional devices to provide information for large numbers at low cost will continue the rapid growth already underway. An individual student will draw on these resources as he plans and pursues his learning and when called for, with the help of appropriate resource persons, he will develop his own independent studies, his own programs of reading, writing, action, and reflection.

Essentially each person will be operating like the creative housewife who supplies herself and her family with a rich, healthful, and varied diet. At first she relies quite heavily on cookbooks and on the advice and example of more experienced cooks who know their way around the kitchen and the market. She continues to consult these resources for new ideas and suggestions but is increasingly independent and in time contributes original creations of her own. The cafeteria has been a good metaphor for recent changes in higher education which give students more choice among ready-to-eat alternatives, tastily prepared and enticingly presented. But the cafeteria assumes that the consumer has no kitchen and doesn't know how to cook, so the supermarket has been proposed, which recognizes that most persons want to prepare their own foods to suit their own tastes and dietary requirements. The supermarket supplies not only foods which are fully prepared and ready-to-eat but also the raw materials which the housewife can put together with nourishing, appetizing, and esthetically appealing results. The young housewife relies almost exclusively on the supermarket at first, but before long she learns about other markets which offer better quality at lower costs. Higher education too will extend beyond the cafeteria and the supermarket into the marketplace itself, capitalizing on all the rich sources of nourishment to be found there.

Dressel and DeLisle examined college catalogs to study curriculum trends from 1957 to 1967 and found substantial changes toward individualized instruction.[1] The percentage of

[1] P. L. Dressel and F. H. DeLisle, *Undergraduate Curriculum Trends* (Washington, D.C.: American Council on Education, 1969).

institutions using six of eight different "developments for individualizing and integrating learning experiences" (advanced placement, honors programs, independent studies, seminars, tutorials, and interim terms) more than doubled in the ten-year period. Each of these developments permits students to work on topics closely tailored to their own interests and to work at their own levels of competence and efficiency. These changes are rapidly becoming more widespread. In 1970, for example, Thompson and Dressel surveyed independent study practices at a representative group of 372 colleges and universities and found that 84 per cent had such programs, a 24 per cent increase over Dressel and DeLisle's previous sample.[2] The number of students who have participated in such programs is still small. Nevertheless, these changes have gathered sufficient momentum and are so consistent with the directions of social change and with the fundamentals of human development that it is almost certain they will become commonplace during the next ten years.

Individualizing the curriculum has broader implications. For example, what are the proper learning media when the "classroom" is any environment that provides learning? Until recently print has reigned unchallenged. Television, film, tape recordings, and computers are upstarts; higher education is still hooked on books. Encounters with print far outweigh all others "for credit." Yet most things are learned more fully, more efficiently, and more permanently when experienced. When the Bible says that Adam knew Eve, it reminds us that "knowing" originally meant much more than the relatively pallid, abstract, and symbolic experience of words.

Knowing requires linking experiences to symbolic representations—words, pictures, numbers, rhythms, melodies—which we can carry with us through time and space. Events

[2] M. M. Thompson and P. L. Dressel, "A Survey of Independent Study Practices," *Educational Record,* Fall 1970, 392–395.

which are not tied to symbolic posts contribute little to education; symbols which have no counterparts in direct or vicarious experiences are hazy and abstract. Verbalizing an experience can expand its meaning, reveal subtleties and implications, suggest relationships with other experiences. But verbalization in the absence of relevant experience is empty. Similarly, the mature learner realizes that while symbolic representations and simulated realities may help him grasp the abstraction, direct experiences provide the flesh, blood, and muscles which bring the bare bones to life. Every week supplies a rich flow of such experiences: work, relationships with friends and family, citizenship and community service activities, recreational pursuits, and the mass media present experiences and opportunities for action pertinent to the major dimensions of personal development. Every community contains untapped resources for intellectual, interpersonal, and occupational development. The person who is integrating educational activities with the rest of his life and who is taking the initiative for his own learning and development will recognize these opportunities and will connect his living with his learning wherever it makes sense.

Programs connecting living and learning and making use of direct experiences are increasing rapidly. Dressel and DeLisle's study revealed a fourfold increase in off-campus and nonresident terms and study abroad. Educational programs based in residence halls jumped from 1.5 per cent to 10.6 per cent; fieldwork experience and community-service programs also increased substantially. Of course, these sharp increases are partly a function of the very low rates in 1957, but there is no questioning the statistics since 1967.

These fundamental changes—increased individual initiative and responsibility and increased use of experience and on-going responsibilities as part of the learning process—will require major shifts in the teacher's role; in teacher-student relationships; in curriculum, teaching, and evaluation; in the role of the residential experience; in the definition of the campus; in governance; and in financing. What is required above all is careful definition of purposes and thorough analyses of the educational conditions and practices which will serve those purposes.

The first pressure for such analyses comes from the skyrocketing costs of education. But high costs are less problematic than low productivity. A major cost of education results from the large number of teachers employed. Education is not quite where agriculture was two hundred years ago, when it took twenty men on the farm to feed one townsman. Nevertheless, the contribution of the individual teacher must be multiplied if the escalating demands for education are to be met. The other major costs stem from our attempts to simulate in the schools the problems and requirements encountered outside. We build scientific laboratories, and we convert persons, problems, and outside conditions into "case studies." We convert cultures into print and film, even when diverse cultures are down the street, around the corner, or within an overnight drive. How much more efficient is it to use available community resources and the direct and responsible relationships they afford us? The result is not only lower educational costs but more effective and powerful learning.

There is a more fundamental and far-reaching reason for thorough consideration of educational purposes and practices. Education has become the principal instrument by which the human species develops its young. Family and community used to be the principal instruments, and schooling played a limited and special role. Now, when from age six to eighteen most children spend as many waking hours in school and pursuing behaviors determined by schools as they spend on all other waking activities combined, and when social changes require that education become a continuing part of adult existence, education is the dominant force shaping contemporary man. Education now creates the image of man we live by—an image that is a self-fulfilling prophecy. Therefore, the future of the world and of man's relationship to it depend on the wisdom of our actions concerning future educational priorities and programs. Sound judgment and wise priorities for action will support the major reorientations in work, in marriage and family living, in relationships with friends and acquaintances, and in citizenship activities, which are required as the center of gravity shifts from a primary concern for survival and the production of material goods to concern for individual expansion and personal development for the realization and enlargement of human potentialities. Misjudgment or misplaced priorities may lead to a new human nature which combines the animal irrationality of primitive man with the materialistic greed and lust of industrial man, powered by the destructive forces which have been released by modern technology. Man's fate and the fate of education are inextricably linked. How the relationship is managed will make all the difference.

Chapter 3

New Values and Faculty Response

Nevitt Sanford

A kind of inhumanity, a willingness to use people in the interest of the social group or institution, runs throughout society today. We find in industry something that is quite comparable to what we see in the university. Industry in this country traditionally is organized according to what is called the mechanical theory of management. You define the work roles, state the relation of one role to another, and require that people adapt themselves precisely to the role requirements, just as in education, students traditionally are presented with a set of curriculum and a set of arrangements with respect to educational procedures, and are expected to adapt themselves accordingly.

When I was at Vassar College during the fifties, I never

heard of students having any complaints about the curriculum. They complained about the food and they began to complain in the late fifties about the parietal rules, but it never occurred to them that it was their part to have any opinions about the curriculum. Sociologists still write about the university in this way, as if it were ordained by nature. It is a system to which individuals must adapt themselves: if they do, they will thereby become acculturated and become full members of the society; if they cannot or will not adapt, it must be because they are pathological. That, however, is not exactly the way students feel today.

"Human relations" were introduced in industry some twenty-five to thirty years ago because managers realized it was becoming increasingly difficult for people to adapt themselves completely to their increasingly specialized work roles; it was realized they needed something to make them a little happier, so they would work better and do what was required. Human relations experts tried to figure out ways to motivate workers, to make them feel satisfaction in belonging to a company, or in the fact that somebody was paying attention to what they did. Comparable to this is the practice on campuses, in the recent past, of letting students have their fun and games or even have something to say about dormitory rules and the like, as long as they didn't tamper with the curriculum.

Today, something in the nature of organic management is just beginning to make inroads into the business community. This is the notion that the individual and his work role constitute a techno-social system, and the whole thing will work better if the individuals who are going to do the work have some say in organizing that work. Studies at a few places where this idea has been adopted show that if you let the workers decide how they are going to go about a task you not only get a more genuine worker morale but a higher production level. In education, this would correspond to arranging educational procedures with actual attention to the needs of students. This is, I think, the burning issue in our society today: Is it possible to change institutions which are organized around the concept of production efficiency in such a way that they can to some extent protect and preserve the individual personality? In general, it seems to me, business, industry, and institutions of higher learning are changing rather slowly—they are not exactly running away with these new ideas. Industry typically responds to pressures toward change with tokenism and public relations activities.

To a very large extent, educational institutions do the same. Despite all of the excitement on college campuses during the last six or eight years—depending on when you think this began (some people think it began in Berkeley in 1964; some think it began with the 1962 publication of *The American College*)—there haven't been many fundamental changes in our great universities. There can be little doubt that the course/unit credit system is generally prettty much as it has been for a great many years. Despite all the excitement at Berkeley, beginning in 1964, I believe that it is fair to say that there have been no changes of any importance in the educational program and structure there. The same is true for all higher education. The fact is that almost everybody in the educational system has a vested interest in things as they are, and each one thinks it would cost him something if any kind of substantial change were to come about. At the same time, students and ethnic minorities are increasing the pressure for change; sooner or later something will have to give.

The basic new value orientation, I suggest, is that young people do not want to fragment themselves or give themselves up in the interest of conforming to educational or work roles. It used to be that a law schol graduate who was going into a firm, quite aware of the fact that he was not in favor of all the goals of the corporation, told himself that he would put in his eight hours a day, do what he was supposed to, earn his money, and lead his life elsewhere. Of course, many young people are still saying that. But a great many are challenging the very proposition that it is necessary to segregate your work life from the rest of yourself in order to have the rewards of a comfortable life in society. It is this same feeling that gives rise to unrest in students who would like a little more attention given to their actual needs and a little less pressure to perform whatever is required to make it in the system. This is, in my view, an irreversible change. It's a new consciousness on the part of students; they will no more return to the rather slavish conformity to educational requirements than a Protestant fundamentalist liberated through his philosophy courses would return to his former fundamentalism. I say irreversibe also because the changes in society to which these things are due—for example, the disappearance of the Horatio Alger myth and the presence of a galloping technology with the affluence that goes with it, the existence of larger corporate systems which pay no attention whatsoever to individuals—go on apace, and they arouse the kind of resistance in individuals that I am talking about.

Interviews with college faculty show that almost all professors—at least those in the San Francisco Bay Area—have felt the impact of the new skepticism or, as some would call it, incivility or rebelliousness. Mervin Freedman says that as early as 1965, at San Francisco State College, he had to endure students' walking out of his classroom in the middle of a lecture, sometimes underlining their point with an expletive.[1] In 1967, he was scheduled to lecture at Stanford and looked forward to talking with students in that genteel setting. The same thing happened as at San Francisco State. He says he still hasn't recovered from the shock.

My own baptism by fire did not occur until the spring of 1968 when I accepted an opportunity to teach at the Unitarian Seminary in Berkeley. When I first had the thought that it might be interesting to teach in a seminary, I went up to look the place over. Since I wanted particularly to look over the students, I arranged a seminar with about a dozen of them. I

[1] Personal communication.

found half-way through that they were in fact looking me over, and it dawned on me that it was quite literally true that the students at this seminary decided who was going to teach there, or at least had rights of refusal in the matter.

Having sweated it out while they decided whether or not I could teach there, I was finally admitted and began giving a seminar in something like "Self and Society." And then I found that the usual ways of proceeding wouldn't do at all, and that I hardly had a chance to say anything. Whereas I had assumed that as in most university courses I would suggest that something be read and the students would read it, these students apparently were reading something else and certainly wanted to discuss something else. In short, I couldn't seem to get a word in edgewise, and we struggled through the term trying to straighten out our relations with each other. The students seemed to be mainly preoccupied with their own development, or their own identity, or their relationships with each other and with the faculty, and so on, whereas I had the somewhat naive idea that we could discuss intellectual matters.

The situation became a bit clearer for me in the winter quarter when a really distinguished theologian came to teach at the school. He had his seminar the first day and almost everybody showed up for it. That evening there was a party at the president's house and I was talking with this old gentleman as he greeted various students. And each time he would say, "I appreciated your remarks in seminar this afternoon." A little later I remarked to a student I knew, "It seems to me the old boy wasn't getting a chance to say very much." He said, "You know what they are doing, don't you? They were giving him your stuff." That was enlightening for me. It appeared that they were willing to learn something from me, but they were not yet ready to let me know that this was the case. The students, of course, become very good ministers, but half-way through the year I was saying to myself, "I wish they could become good ministers without being so hard on their teachers."

Whereas most teachers have had or soon will have experiences of this kind, not all respond in the same way. My chief concern here is with several different patterns of response, with some of their consequences and determinants. I base myself upon intensive interviews with 300 faculty members carried out by my Wright Institute colleagues at seven institutions in the San Francisco Bay Area.[2] I have the benefits also of an important unpublished paper by Jeff Goldsmith (Reed College, 1970, and now a graduate student in sociology at the University of Chicago) in which he analyzes in sociological and ethnographic terms the cultural polarization that led to an ugly "tuition boycott" or strike at his college. We shall see that both analyses offer similar conclusions.

Michael Bloom and Norbert Ralph of The Wright Institute have separately described three patterns of faculty reaction to the new forms of student behavior: first, sticking strictly—even rigidly—to the pattern of values and behavior toward students that existed before the appearance of student unrest on the campus; second, radical accommodation to the new student values and behavior, almost an identification with students; and third, integration of the new values into a scheme broad enough and flexible enough to embrace the new without total rejection of the old. In a general way the first two types correspond to factions of Reed College faculty involved in the polarization described by Jeff Goldsmith. The majority of the faculty held firmly the "traditional ideology of education" in accord with which Reed was founded; that is, a heavy accent on performance in strictly academic subjects, with no frills but with much formal and informal faculty-student contact; the traditional course-unit-grade system within a totally academic institution. There was, in Goldsmith's words, "an application

[2] This work is the basis for a forthcoming book by Mervin Freedman and associates. Unpublished working papers are available through The Wright Institute.

of the Protestant ethic to academic life." Over the years Reed attracted enough students who were suitably motivated for this kind of education that, despite a high drop-out rate, the college was able to build a solid reputation for academic excellence. After 1963, however, Reed students, like very bright and sophisticated students everywhere, began to show signs of unrest and protest, and gradually the college began to assume a different image in the public mind, that of a lively, avant-garde place where students could do their own thing. Without any reduction of admission standards or academic requirements, Reed began to acquire what was to become a substantial and highly visible "beat" subculture, one that has been called the "cult of experience" or "Consciousness III." According to Goldsmith, by January 1970 the student body included a heavy admixture of students who wanted and expected of the college not only a sound academic education but everything necessary to their pleasure, security, identity, social conscience—their souls.

Reed also acquired during the 1960s a number of new faculty members who, though they were willing to work within a traditional structure, may not have held the traditional values in the same way as did the older faculty. At any rate, in the contests that soon developed between the students with new values and the established authority of the college, a good proportion of these faculty members sided with the students. When it became known that the appointments of some of these faculty would not be renewed for 1971–1972, a group of students began planning a tuition boycott and the fat was in the fire.

I would assume that most, but not all, of Goldsmith's "traditionalists" would show the pattern of response which my colleagues and I, on the basis of interviews, have called "stand pat-ism." The most essential characteristic of this pattern is that the professor, in the face of changing reality, clings to the system of thought and action to which he has grown accustomed. The more inportunate the new demands upon him, the more totally he rejects the new values, the more rigidly he reaffirms his longstanding position. Instead of adapting to change he seeks to interpret events in a way that will be in keeping with his preexisting scheme. Although the stand-patter continues to present himself with characteristic self-confidence and authority, in reality he is perplexed and threatened. He may fear that all he has worked for is being undermined. He knows that his prestige has diminished and that he has to struggle to maintain his self-esteem. But he does not change his way of teaching unless to reassert his authority, to show his complete mastery of the facts, or to isolate himself further from the students.

Students respond negatively. They are inclined to see his authoritarian ways as a sign of weakness; they are less and less inclined to model themselves upon him as a person; and very often they are not looking for the kind of technical competence he has to offer. Their rejection may lead to more authoritarianism.

Origin of Response Patterns

It is helpful to view professors in the light of a theoretical model of development in the academic setting. One begins with the quite logical notion that professors develop as individuals in much the same way that other people do. Their development is progressive and is marked by distinct stages, which are only loosely related to chronological age. A particularly important stage is the achievement of a sense of competence in one's discipline or specialty. The ways in which this developmental task is approached and accomplished depend, of course, on what has gone before in the individual life. It depends, for example, on whether the professor was, as a child, "isolated" or "social." Perhaps it is unsurprising to discover that the overwhelming majority of the professors in The Wright Institute sample were isolated children. Indeed, half of those interviewed in one liberal arts college were only children. Whether prodigies or plodders they learned early to enjoy being rewarded by adults for academic achievement and they learned late, if at all, to participate in the rough and tumble of campus politics. The mischievous and sometimes disobedient "social" children who were to become professors were relatively late in discovering their academic potentialities and, though they are likely to wind up in charge of the important committees and to relate easily to students outside of classes, they have a hard time getting over the feeling that they may not be doing the right thing in the classroom.

Until he has achieved academic competence the professor is not ready to pass on to the stage of self-discovery, in which he gives attention to other abilities, interests, and aspirations, and so expands his personality. Even when a professor is ready to change, however, he finds that he has made commitments and must defend what he has done, while also dealing with the expectations of family and colleagues who, often at some pain, have grown used to him as he is. Our experience is in line with Lewin's finding that it usually takes some "group decision" to sustain a change.[3] Ideally, self-discovery is followed by discovery of others: as in Erik Erikson's formulation of stages, identity is followed by intimacy and generativity.[4] Now the professor is prepared to use all of his skills in genuine relations with other people; he may find it comfortable and enjoyable to take a father role with some students—those who can tolerate or accept it.

The stand-pat professor is, most commonly, I believe, in the developmental stage of establishing or maintaining a sense of competence. His concern is mainly with the approval and recognition of his professional colleagues and his status within

[3] K. Lewin, "Group Decision and Social Change," in T. M. Newcomb and E. L. Hartley (Eds.), *Readings in Social Psychology*. New York: Holt, Rinehart, and Winston, 1947.

[4] E. H. Erikson, *Childhood and Society*. New York: Norton, 1950.

the academic world. Thus it is that his self-definition and self-respect depend heavily upon his adherence to the traditional academic beliefs and ways. This adherence is also a matter of conscience. He regards the academic value orientation as a guide to life and would feel guilty if he failed to act in accord with it. Profesors differ in the degree to which the stability and integration of their personality depends upon the stability of the academic culture, but the extent of this dependence is shown by the fact that serious external or internal attacks on the university or college are experienced and reacted to as if they were threats to the personality. The traditional value orientation is assimilated and held to in different ways. In one case it may be a matter of conformity, the professor changing as the external climate changes; in another case the values may have been assimilated in accord with the professor's best judgment, and so be deeply based in his personality.

The academic culture is not, of course, exactly of one piece; it varies somewhat from one institution to another and, slowly, over time. It may embody a measure of concern for the individual student and his intellectual development, and this aspect might be particularly meaningful to some teachers. There are teachers, for example, who as undergraduates experienced intellectual awakening at the hands of a particular devoted instructor and who now want to be that kind of teacher themselves. Such teachers find the new rebelliousness or lack of deference on the part of students particularly hard to take. Why should they, who really care about students, be subjected to insults and distrust? The case is different from that of the professor who embraced the academic values when he was in graduate school. Since his concern is with his subject and his discipline and the structure which sustains them, and since he knows he is right, the indifference, skepticism, or opposition of students may be a matter for some regret but nothing to be deeply disturbed about.

The second type of professor with whom we are concerned deals with the new values by embracing them and substantially modifying his frame of reference. He may make a total commitment to the new values and become radical with a vengeance. Sometimes it appears that his new orientation has the same absolutism as did his old one; sometimes it seems he feels he has at last found himself. Or it seems that the students have asked "What is the relevance of this?" or "Why should I know this?" and, having no answer, he has joined them in their search. In any case he becomes antiestablishment, or even anti-intellectual. Students who espouse the new values become his major reference group, and sometimes he identifies himself with them—in the psychodynamic sense of this term. Students generally accept this type of professor at first, and he may become popular. They feel he understands them. He relates to them as a peer, shares their interests, makes friends among them. But they soon see that he is searching for answers in the same way they are. They can accept him as a peer but not as a guide; they see that there is little to be learned from one who regards his past as a waste of time.

At first glance it appears that these professors have attained a sense of competence and are now embarking on a voyage of self-discovery. In some cases this is genuine. The young professor has performed brilliantly in the terms of his discipline and specialty and risen rapidly. Faced with the strong appeal of the new values he begins to test them in action; but at the same time he begins a period of soul-searching which may end with an integration of the old and the new. More often, it seems, he embraces the new values with as little self-insight, as little self-actualization, as marked his acceptance of the old ones. Perhaps he came along too fast, as universities are wont to make able people do, defining himself too early and too narrowly in terms of his specialty without benefit of an education that could have prepared the way for self-discovery. He has reaped the rewards of rapid advancement and a clear sense of professional identity and now for the first time has to confront serious questions of value. He wants now to discover himself but is starting from nearly the same point as his students. Like them he feels that the system has let him down and like them he is against it, but he is hard put to know what to build in its place. Like most professors, he has never given serious thought to a theory of education.

When this professor's acceptance of the traditional value orientation, which he is now throwing over, is absolute, one suspects that it was somehow problematic in the first place. Perhaps he accepted the system under pressure, and while conforming strictly to its demands barely controlled his rebellious impulses and was barely conscious that he was violating parts of himself. Or perhaps he was always conscious of his alienation from the academic community and welcomes the opportunity to liberate himself from it. What is probably quite common in professors of this type is a remnant of their cynical adaptation to graduate school. They "played the game" without any genuine commitment of self, enjoyed the benefits of outward conformity, and are now coping with bad conscience.

One of the most poignant cases is that of the young professor who is driven into the student camp by his ambitious and rigidly traditional department. Concerned by student unrest on the campus and enjoying good relations with students, he believes he may serve the community by becoming a member of, for example, the student-faculty disciplinary committee. This takes much time, and though he continues to publish in his specialty, his rate of publication declines. After a couple of years of this the department has no use for him and he is out instead of up. A spirited young man might regard this as quite sufficient reason for joining the rebels.

The third type of professor, as I have said, reacts to student skepticism neither by rigid reassertion of his existing scheme nor by radical change but by integrating the two. He is not upset by the student skepticism because he has remained skeptical himself. He has useful and enjoyable guidelines but does not regard them as absolute or good for everybody. He is willing to change his beliefs if he finds more satisfactory ones. He wants to share what has given him satisfaction and he believes he can learn by discussing alternative views. Far from neglecting the facts or technical aspects of his field he sees them as integral to the studies that he loves. He rather dislikes the role of authority but is willing to assume it when necessary. He believes students might well learn something from his experience, but he does not expect them to accept what is not relevant to their lives.

This professor is not an especially dominant force in either direction and may well be in the background during periods of unrest, but he endures. Students in his classes do not abandon their skepticism, but they come to see that he is deriving satisfaction from his style and outlook, that he has dealt successfully with some of the questions they face that he might—at least for the time being—be a suitable model. Self-contained, he is cordial toward but not intimate with students. The key fact about this professor is that *he* is still developing. He is still incorporating his past within himself and entertaining conceptions of what he might yet become. It is his experience in development and as a developing person that he wants to share with students, and what they see, however dimly, can be useful to them.

This professor's sense of himself as a developing person owes much to fortunate development in the past. His definition of himself as an academic man has come from his own inner needs. He is an academic man because he has found in the forms of academia suitable means for self-actualization rather than a source of identity where none existed before. In short, he does largely what he wants to do rather than reacting to the demands of a role. He respects the academic norms because they serve him and others reasonably well but he does not regard them as absolute. In the terms of our developmental scheme this professor is most open to development because, compared to the other two types, he has already developed the most. His discovery of self probably began early—when he gave thought to what he was to become, probably trying several alternatives—and now he will usually be found to have more than one string to his bow. We have to assume that a sense of competence was attained long since, and that his renewed self-discovery prepared the way for discovery of others.

Changing Academic Culture

When we turn to the question of how matters might be changed, how teaching might be improved, and how colleges and universities might become more humane and enjoyable places, we might easily find ourselves at a loss, for the analysis suggests that we must change both personality and culture and that the two are so intimately bound together that we can hardly think of changing one without changing the other.

I am going to suggest, however, that we summon new courage and resources and see what can be done about changing academic culture. First I need to say something more about the nature of this beast. Academic culture is a set of shared ways and views designed to make professors' ills more bearable, (for example, to contain their anxieties and uncertainties about their competence as teachers) and to prevent any flight to "others they know not of." I will not undertake to describe the whole academic culture here, but only wish to indicate some features that might have to be changed if college teaching is to improve.

For example, professors often identify with their discipline or specialty rather than with the role of teacher. They respect the norms concerning how much time one may properly spend with students or how much interest in students one may display. In most institutions these norms are pretty low: if one becomes a popular teacher, he courts the danger of being ostracized by colleagues. Similarly he must beware of "popularism" lest he give away too much of the mystery upon which support of his discipline depends. One should not in conversation with colleagues or other profesisonals go beyond the bounds of one's own specialty. If something outside of one's specialty comes up for discussion one always defers to other specialists, although this puts an end to the conversation. And one should always exhibit devotion to the highest standards in matters of appointments, promotions, and admission of students. Let somebody else suggest that a risk be taken in particularly interesting cases.

It all seems pretty grim—as indeed it is. One might be inclined to think that we academic men would be as happy as kings since we are fundamentally free to read and study and look into whatever we like, always have interesting colleagues to talk with, and are surrounded by eager students waiting to get the word. Instead we find in our institutions of higher learning widespread unhappiness and cynicism, and the academic culture seems to decree that it ought not be otherwise. Since the faculty member is devoted to such high purposes—the pursuit of which is constantly interfered with by people who do not understand—it would seem almost immoral to take any pleasure in what one does.

This culture, and its accompanying lack of exposure to educational questions, prevent communication among professors who are interested in students and deprive the individual teacher of means for evaluating his work. With no terms for describing student development, without even a perspective from which the student can be seen as a person, the teacher of undergraduates is denied the most elementary satisfaction of professional activity; that is, seeing some desirable results from planned action. This is not to say that the professor receives no psychological rewards from his teaching, but these rewards are random and unsystematic, when they could be—if teaching were placed in a suitable professional context—regular and durable.

The liberation of professors from academic culture can be attained through the achievement of three interrelated goals: greater self-awareness and recognition of what being a professor means—philosophies, objectives, and styles of teaching; familiarity with alternate ways of attaining their objectives; and recognition of the legitimacy of being interested in students and taking satisfaction from work with them. Of these goals the first is the most basic. If the professor's alienation from himself and his classroom work can be overcome, it will be easy for him to see new possibilities in the classroom and in work with students as individuals. Increased awareness leads to seeing students in a new light. The more familiar the professor is with his own feelings—his anxieties and misgivings as well as his satisfactions—the greater his ability to understand what students are thinking and feeling, and the greater the latter, the more conscious of his classroom behavior and the more able to evaluate his work he will be.

Teachers and teaching are almost never discussed in the way I have just illustrated—neither on campuses nor in scientific or popular writing about education. This largely defines our problem and sets our task. We must expose, and begin the process of breaking up this "conspiracy of silence." In our work along these lines we proceed in three ways: conduct intensive and comprehensive interviews with faculty members; use analysis of these interviews to lead discussions among groups of teachers; and observe teachers in their classrooms and then analyze their work with them.

Interviews center on issues which, as we know from experience, are deeply relevant to the work and the lives of college professors. All of the questions are open-ended. This frees the professor to dwell on what is uniquely relevant and spares him the feeling that he is being classified or that what he has to say is being cataloged according to somebody else's preconceptions. In the conduct of the interviews the professor's confidence in the interviewer is most important. This rests most fundamentally on the latter's actual interest and compassion and on the fact that he has no axe to grind. Apart from these considerations, the interviewer who comes to the professor from outside the latter's department or school has certain distinct advantages: he is not a competitor, nor an authority; unlike the professor's colleagues and professional associates this interviewer is in no position, nor has he the inclination, to hold what the professor says against him. More, the interviewer is there to talk about subjects in which the professor has deep interest but which he never has a chance to talk about, except possibly when he or she is at home with his wife or her husband.

Almost without exception those interviewed have said they enjoyed the experience and benefited from it. It is my firm conviction that they do indeed benefit in ways suggested above: they are given a chance to reflect on important matters that have been little in their attention; they do a certain amount of personal stock-taking; they discover—often with considerable relief—that it is possible to talk about troublesome and revealing aspects of their experiences with students. In short, a process leading to increasing self-awareness is set in motion.

To increase the likelihood that the benefits of the individual interview will be sustained, an attempt is made to stimulate campus-wide (or, in large universities, department-wide or school-wide) conversations and discussion about the program and the issues it raises. For one thing, by interviewing a relatively high proportion of the teachers in a given college, department, or professional school—all of whom are approached directly, not through the good offices of the administration—it is highly likely that conversations about the interviews and their content will spring up spontaneously. In addition, after all the interviews at a given school have been completed, and the material has been studied, group discussions are scheduled at the institutions. Sometimes in small groups and sometimes in meetings to which the whole faculty is invited, tentative findings that are intrinsically interesting and discussable are reported and the meetings are conducted in ways that invite discussion. If the teachers present have not already discovered that their anxieties are widely shared and that there are indeed viable alternatives to their own ways of doing things, they often do so at this point.

The idea of self-study is, of course, an old one in the world of higher education. There have been many self-studies in recent years, more than a few of which turned out to be expensive exercises in self-congratulation. Rarely have they resulted in significant changes. In what I am proposing the agency of changes lies in the process of self-study itself—not in some academic body that makes up its mind to do something or, more likely, not to do something, after the so-called facts are in. The procedure is based on the assumption that professors are human, that they have needs and aspirations that are not fulfilled under present arrangements but which, when they have been brought fully into awareness, can be fulfilled—without loss to other values—under different arrangements. I have no doubt that a particular institution could bring in a "team" to carry out the procedures described here and thereby accomplish more in the way of improving teaching—and at less expense—than is accomplished by present efforts to recruit teachers of known effectiveness or to supply financial rewards for superior teaching.

This, of course, would be only a modest beginning, but it is in what I am sure is the right direction; that is, toward making our institutions of higher learning more human. It is not only students but millions of people who work in large organizations who are alienated from their work and suffer from the impersonality of their surroundings. It is ironic that our colleges and universities, which are supposed to teach us how to live and which could be models of human communities, tend to go the way of other bureaucracies. There are graduate schools of social science that seem perfectly willing to dehumanize their students in order to turn them into scientists who will see to it that we eventually have a society in which no one need be dehumanized. We owe to students, I think, the effective critique of this irrational future-orientation. The time to treat people as human beings is *now,* and the place is where we are, in the college or in the schools and departments of the university. This goes for the faculty as well as for the students.

My analysis puts the emphasis on change in consciousness. This is not to deny the importance of change in the academic structure; it is merely to put first things first, for the best-laid plans for academic reform will go awry unless they accord with faculty attitudes and wishes. It is the faculty, as we all know, who have the ultimate power. Finally, I would like to emphasize that I am not talking about change for its own sake; I do have in mind models for the future. Their delineation has not been my task here; I would like to stress, however, what I think is an essential ingredient of any good model: since the students' development—which is the fundamental aim of education—depends heavily upon the development of the faculty there must be arrangements, both conceptual and practical, for the latter to occur. I am reverting now to the third type of professor, who could deal with his students' skepticism because he was at home with his own.

Here it is well to remind ourselves of an old but often neglected principle of the mental health field: doctors and patients, welfare workers and clients, parents and children need each other; together each of these pairs constitutes a unity or dynamic system. The fate of the patient, client, or child depends a great deal on the *kind* of need he satisfies in those responsible for his care. There have been studies showing without doubt that back-wards exist in state hospitals, and the blind are kept in a dependent state largely to satisfy the needs of care-givers for power and a sense of worth. On the other side, sensitive psychotherapists have often reported that the patients they helped the most were the ones who helped *them* the most—those who aided self-discovery in an important way.

Teachers who are honest with themselves will admit, I think, that the era of student protest has taught us how much we have relied upon authoritarian structures and methods and, of course, upon submissive students. But if pathology in the relationship I have mentioned is a product of interaction between those involved, so also is development. If students are developing, the faculty must develop too, and if the faculty wish to develop their students they will do most by taking actions that express and promote their own development.

Chapter 4

The Name of the Game Is the Student

Sally Whelan Cassidy

Our colleges should enable the student to take charge of his own education as rapidly as possible and to chart his own course ever more responsibly, carefully, and sensibly. The teacher should make occasional visits in order to engage the student in chats which might lead him to a new level of conversation or a different kind of effort. My concern is how the student can make use of a college and work with the staff and the staff with him in the pursuit of his own learning. Corporate and personal relationships in various combinations are the ingredients of collegial life. This is a very complex set of interactions. Much turns on our definition of the student, on our ideas of how learning takes place, and on how we place ourselves in our corporate responsibility as a college. It is not enough to say simply: Let us all be prostudent; let us fan all available flames and succor, nourish, and encourage. We also have to articulate anew the decision-making apparatus of the college, namely the admissions policy, grading policy, policy about incompletes, policy about choice of major, and policy about appropriate cadences of sequences.

If we do not change and coordinate the academic apparatus, we are telling the students: You take the risk, and we hope to God you make it, but you are taking the risk on your own and if your end product looks like something we can recognize, fine. If not, that is your worry. But if we take the students seriously and affirm: It is their life, their responsibility, their intellect, their zeal, their discipline, then we have to see to it that we can back them up, that we can legitimize their efforts, that we can explain their rationale to the outside world, whether it be graduate school, employer, draft board, or anyone else. For example, at Monteith, a student is held to a strict ordering of 50 per cent of his courses spread out over a four-year period and is told to use the other 50 per cent to explore, test himself, develop skills, and pursue particular interests. We ask the student to recognize his own coherence and to work out his own rationale. He may have to try to organize his work several times, have to rethink his rationale, because we do not go along with just anything. But when the student's intention is clarified, we recognize it as a whole and are prepared to support his unique constellation of interests.

Even when we prescribe a senior essay to be developed over three quarters, we are trying to give the student a chance at the end of his career to produce a document, manuscript, painting, or perhaps some music, which is his best, most competent achievement. If he wants to go to graduate school or to a conservatory, we urge him to send this, his most mature and skillful work along with his transcript. Then, in our letter of recommendation, we can point not only to that transcript but also to that best example.

Another responsibility involved in helping a student

take hold of his own life is to help him perceive what the college is all about, how it is orchestrated, and what its rules are. The student is expected to achieve some insight into the inner articulations of these rules. We must endeavor to give him some notion of what we are after. We must be prepared to share our own notions about what is out there: to act as interlocutor and a resource person. We cannot simply say or imply, You will get your neck broken there. Rather, we must say: In that particular course you should allow yourself enough time and discipline yourself sharply whereas in this other course, you can safely freewheel. Let us discuss, too, which professors are open to challenges from the floor and which, if any, prefer challenges to be made in writing and documented to the hilt. Some required courses are taught in very doctrinaire fashion and yet must be gotten through; insight into pedagogical styles can help a student to persevere even in an antiintellectual setting. Elsewhere, some sense of epistemology, of the history of ideas, and of the competing schools of thought represented in a department may be needed to help the beginning student make his way in otherwise mystifying and disheartening situations.

This approach may seem very demanding, even risky. However, I would say this kind of effort is still not enough if we are to be maximally useful to our students, particularly to those who have not been brought up in academe. To us the student is a potential, and soon real, peer: a peer in the sense of a person whose intellect, freedom, energy, speculations, and hunches matter, not a peer in the sense of accumulated learning or of know-how.

How can we actualize this relationship? We can do so by giving students a chance to sense how someone who is the full-blown holder of the title of artist, historian, sociologist, or mathematician actually operates. Let the student see some of the workings of that operation, see us with a desk, or six desks, spread out with papers, trying to get our materials into some sort of order. Let him see us not only in the classroom but also as we are trying to write up some of our findings, as we are trying to make sense of apparently divergent evidence, as we are enjoying or annoyed by the latest issue of our favorite journal. In other words, let him get a rounded notion of the activities of the full-fledged intellectual and not limit him to inferring it from our classroom performance. He needs a good deal of "come with me and let us take a look," a lot of "let us get together and work this out another setp." I am not speaking of hand-holding or paternalism but of work, thinking aloud, and being visible in ways other than our most Olympian, our surest, and most polished.

In such a setting, the student can begin to gain some idea of whether a particular discipline is for him. He may be intrigued by the questions but hate the work involved in their resolution. He may prefer simply to use that discipline as an avocation and keep up with it in *Scientific American.* Or he may discover that he has more of a flair for another discipline whose work has a different rhythm or a different mathematical component. All of us have some kind of arduous work to do, but students have difficulty sorting disciplines out. If they are to become genuine seekers, develop truly active intellects, and become truly responsible for their own agenda, we must show them more of our lives than the common factors of classroom, lectures, and offices.

I would not advocate any approach which does not put students in a position where they can see, touch, and taste the decisions, the sparks, the urgency, the curiosity, and the joy of discovering something. For example, we must avoid saying: Here is the big picture, and I will show you ten blow-ups of particular aspects of it—whether it be a river, an institution, or a King's decision. A large-scale survey filled out with a few examples only provides the student with a vocabulary and a sketched map of somebody else's property, someone else's territory. Even the sketch belongs to someone else and the student cannot rearrange it. A crucial part of the vicarious experience

I am advocating is that the student can, at least hypothetically, consider other arrangements of the data or new, untreated questions. The survey-type experience precludes free inquiry by its encyclopedic and misleadingly exact nature.

Our first task then is to raise the standard of student participation. We must take into consideration their preparation, the size of the class, the local opportunities (or paucity of materials). Above all, we must give the student access to the intellectual at work, whether he be artist, scientist, psychologist, or geographer. Let the student witness the excitement the man experiences and the price he pays for it. If the student witnesses the discovery process often enough, he will come to see for himself that the university experience includes more than worries of "What can I fill my nine o'clock slot with?" or "How do I meet my natural science requirement?" Rather, he will realize that he has a limited number of chances to try out ideas, test himself, and become acquainted with several unknown fields of knowledge.

Our detailed longitudinal study of Monteith students in their fourth year in college [1] revealed that it is very important for a student to take hold of his own learning by meeting an instructor in his freshman year whom he still describes as the most meaningful among the whole faculty upon graduation. Early contact with scholars, people who care about the life of the mind, apparently enables the student to test out other alternatives all along the way. It is not the same thing for the student to meet a meaningful person in his junior year. We have arrived at this conclusion by tracing a large number of indices of intellectual performance: testing scores, graduate record exams, the date of graduation, ability to perform in diverse academic settings. On all these indices, students who

[1] S. W. Cassidy and others, *Impact of a High-Demand College in a Large University on Working Class Youth,* Final Report, Project no. 5-0818, contract no. OE-0-10-046. Washington, D.C.: Office of Education, 1968, Vol. 1, pp. 198, 407ff.

had met a meaningful person early in their university career did much better; it was as if they had been in full possession of themselves throughout. Equally bright persons who met their meaningful professor later somehow never mastered the university, and did not take hold as thoroughly.

What we propose, then, to the newly arrived students is a crucial matter. The first year can be considered an apprenticeship, like a novitiate for a monk, where the student must demonstrate that he can read and write just as the monk demonstrates he can pray and obey. This approach differs sharply from the exhilarating experience of saying: This is for me. The university is my sort of oyster, and I like the taste of seafood. In the first year, we are asking the student to make a tremendous number of important decisions, often prematurely. The foreign language he chooses, the level of difficulty of the science course he enrolls for, the particular professor he chooses (very often, I suspect, in terms of a time slot) could have a massive influence on subsequent choices. His advisors may be urging him to select a major when he has scarcely enough input to make a meaningful choice. But the first year may also be a time of freedom to select only among trivia. This was my own fate as a freshman. I, in all innocence, took a counselor's advice and found myself scheduled into gigantic classes which the administration wanted filled. I realized only much later that part of my student responsibility was to be a skilled consumer, undertaking to puzzle out that a professor may be brilliant in course A and routinely dull in course B. I also learned that it was better to wait for instructor X to come back from sabbatical rather than take the particular course from other instructors who were presently assigned to it. One such lesson I learned as a young teacher at the University of Chicago from my student Carl Werthman, who, as a professor's son, came to the university already aware of much of the actual agenda of any university. He had not been allowed to take a course taught by Gerhardt Meyer, a magnificent teacher of history. I remember him red-faced in his indignation, coming to me, and saying, "It cost my father money. It cost me money. I want the best education possible. I want Gerhardt Meyer." And, by heavens, he wrangled his way into Meyer's class. Who but a professor's son would so early in the game have that instrumental sense of the university, the college, the course, the discipline, the teachers—of his needs and to a certain extent his right to insist on the best?

I have seen freshman programs which were primarily aimed at what I would call incorporation, giving the students an inner sense of the university or college's functioning, of the collegial relations, of an academic heritage. I have seen this done at the College of the University of Chicago where the university literally took months explaining to students its testing policy, admissions policy, the rationale for courses being organized in a particular way, the reasons why things were done in the sophomore year and not in the junior year, and saying in effect: This is how *we* work and how *you* fit in. Should we not ask ourselves: How soon does the student get a chance to say "we," a "we" that includes the faculty and not simply other freshmen. One of the great advantages of a learning situation is the happiness of having so much wealth available to one and so many people who care. Part of the sadness, and I think part of the anguish, is not knowing how to talk to these people, not knowing how to obtain access, not knowing how to unlock the door, and not yet knowing the timetable, and the agenda. How does a student communicate his new realization that he is a member of the body, an integral part of that academic unity?

The next big issue I would like to raise is the quality of student life or student culture. Our first Monteith graduating class only had a hundred fifteen members. We could visualize almost all of them quite clearly; each of them had achieved a perceptibly unique answer to his educational needs. Yet our research revealed that among these few people, there were six distinct, identifiable student cultures, three of which were almost independent of staff.[2] One such group consisted of professionals who were busy meeting their pre-med requirements and seemed to postpone their humane development, perhaps until after marriage when their wives would drag them to concerts. Clearly, these people had their agenda firmly in mind, a clear-cut vocation that wants no self-scrutiny or gratuitous chit-chat. I think students have a right to a clear-cut vocation, although I have seen only a few admirable cases of doctor-humanists. We almost too routinely alluded to William Carlos Williams in our few discussions with these students.

Then we found students who had such an array of well placed, bright friends that they did not need teacher mediators. They had friends in every niche in the university. They were *the* in-group. At Chicago, these were the professors' children. At Wayne, they were graduates of the top high schools in the city. They coalesced into a natural clique. Within this group, word quickly got around as to who the good teacher was, what the new rule on procedure meant, how to circumvent a particular requirement, which professor was on leave next quarter, or what student jobs were opening up. They handled most of their practical problems themselves, they were their own experts, and were often useful informants to new teachers or to the few nonclique students they happened to encounter.

The last of the three groups which held themselves aloof from the staff was the ethnic students who lacked teachers of similar background with whom they could identify: Poles, for instance. We didn't succeed in recruiting a Polish staff member. As the Polish students saw it, nobody could safely act as their interlocutor. These students, I suspect, were kept on a starvation diet for two or three years until, one at a time, they managed to find someone on the staff they could talk to. These late discoverers of meaningful faculty members were bright people but timid and too ready to rule themselves out of the action.

[2] Cassidy and others, pp. 239ff.

The other three student cultures also differed enormously among themselves: campus leaders and politicos, highly intellectual types, and those we might categorize as friendly do-gooders. Members of each clique called on teachers very differently. It was fascinating, for instance, to see that the brightest students from professional backgrounds did not wish to have a teacher as a model. They wanted him to be a good pedagogue whom they could respect as an intellectual who knew his business. "Friendship and fraternizing are fine, but no nonsense; I want a good teacher." The contrary was true for students from working-class families (and we had a substantial proportion of these at Monteith). Models were strongly desired. A student from the working-class background often had nobody close to him who had ever been anything other than a butcher, a cop, a fireman, or an automobile mechanic. Often, the only educated people he had any familiarity with were priests and nuns. He desperately needed models, and so when asked if there were any staff member around he would like to be like, he would answer "Yes, indeed." The faculty was the only tangible manifestation of the reality of the intellectual life he was discovering to be such fun but had no idea of what it might be like to live. Hence, models were crucial for him.

Other students were gifted and lazy. What sort of teacher was most meaningful to them? Who helped them make it through school and get all those assignments done? They chose the teacher who, they thought of as open and tolerant, informal and available socially: the teacher who let them do their own pacing, who agreed to their initially bizarre solutions but who, simultaneously, kept expressing an interest in their work and a concern that they get on with their papers.

Thus, we found three clusters of characteristics in meaningful teachers: the professional intellectual; the model ("This is what it's like to be an astronomer"; and those who endlessly played the Socratic role ("Where are you at, Johnny, what do you see out there?)". This latter group was simultaneously able to move in a given field from any point of entry (they reminded me of particle-traces in a cloud chamber) and able to reconstitute the entire field from virtually any vantage point. This last ability is, what makes teaching fun for many of us. It is exhausting, but it is fun, and it gives the student a sense of the whole, a sense that he has lots of room and a great many challenges. More than anything else, some students need a wide open, the-world-is-their-oyster approach.

To recapitulate: (1) The freshman year is tremendously important, tremendously important for early contact with a staff member, a contact of high enough caliber to make the rest of the student's career in college. Incidentally, we discovered that the meaningful staff member was not necessarily a specialist in the area of a student's intellectual vocation. A young natural scientist can go to a philosopher or a budding social scientist can be beholden to a historian of science. The crucial person is someone a student feels free to check back with throughout his career. (2) Student cultures are more alive, more diverse, more resilient than we might imagine. We repeatedly found that the students could be trusted to bear a large part of the burden of educating each other and in so doing call forth separate and diverse qualities in their peers.

Still, I cannot overstress the importance of the student-teacher relationship. We should have enough types of people, enough styles in the staff, so that many kinds of students can have their needs met. If a range of professors is provided, students do come alive and do take hold of themselves. In our research, we made a final test of this hypothesis to make sure of our results. We took graduates, parceled out some of their key characteristics, and reviewed all of our findings on outcomes (test scores, success in diverse educational settings, prompt graduation, and so on). We tested alternative hypotheses such as the impact of excellence in high school, the impact of college-educated parents, and the impact of high scores on entrance tests. We wanted to know how these initial advantages compare with that of making early contact with a professor who is seen as open to dialogue, a potential model, someone who can be talked to and who deserves respect as an individual.[3] The results put us in a good position to say that students are unthinkable without teachers just as teachers are unthinkable without their students. Apparently, we matter very much to each other. We matter as human beings, as accessible models, and in all sorts of other ways. Our problem then is: How do we turn the college and university into the kind of place where students can liberate themselves, the kind of place students can fully and freely use? Can we liberate the student without killing the professor?

In the program at Monteith, twenty-five staff members have carried prime responsibility for about eight hundred students. Our records show that of these twenty-five staff members, six carried the overwhelming proportion of the burden. These six staff members made themselves unbelievably available in several different ways. Some were skilled in as many as eight languages. Every time I had a difficult paper and failed to understand what the student was saying, I would bring it to one particular colleague and sure enough, he would understand it. Armed with his miraculously perceptive interpretation of the student's intent, I could return to that student and we could move on to the next step. This marvelously versatile man was able and willing to understand and reconstruct another person's stance. Another of the six (I had the impression he never slept) could spend endless successions of evenings with students. Still another held office hours as frequently as from nine to five every day of the week and was willing to schedule meetings on weekends, and in addition had a marvelous aptitude for manipulating the university system by well-placed phone calls. Many, many skills these six people had, and the rest of us could do our bit because they carried so much. I suspect that in a staff that is

[3] Cassidy and others, pp. 410ff.

enthusiastic about what it is doing, is free to build its own programs, and has responsive students, there probably always are people such as our six at Monteith. Our problem is, of course, to ensure their survival. One might ask: Is this not exploitation? I do not think so. Is it necessary for some professors to do manifestly more than others? I think so. *Everybody* does not have to do *everything* in order for students to find *somebody* who responds to them specially.

The red tape can be also eliminated. If I have to check with the department chairman, who has to check with the academic dean, who turns to a faculty committee, I would say: "Forget it. Students don't have that kind of patience, and I am not sure we should encourage them to bear such delaying procedures." As you know, students are likely to have a headlong interest, and if a professor cannot catch it while it flows, we are in trouble. Putting the faculty in a position to seize such moments of learning means trusting them. The errors incidental to such trust are worthwhile in order to reap the tremendous benefits of immediately encouraging the students. In order to minimize errors in judgment, the faculty needs primarily to be given time to rest, reflect, and retool itself. One of the ways by which one might keep the faculty alive would be to have a sabbatical leave of one-half year every three years rather than a full year after six years of labor. This arrangement might be a practical and humane method of coping with fatigue and the need for self-renewal, perhaps more effective in the long run than simply tapping the greater energies of teaching assistants for the short haul. Linear programing and technology may do wonders in helping eliminate rote chores, but clearly some way has to be found which permits the staff to make themselves fully available to the masses of students we have decided it is our duty to educate. But these are the nuts and bolts. The essential thing is to change the emphasis, to reverse what has become tradition, and to let the student be responsible for his own learning.

Chapter 5

Alternative Pathways to Liberal Education

Morris T. Keeton

Mickey McCleery, professor of political science, interrupted his colleague, Barry Hollister, who was preparing for a class. Mickey was obviously in distress and wanted to "talk it out" at once. He thrust a paper into Hollister's hand, asked him to read it then and there but refused to say what the problem was. In the middle of page eight, Hollister broke off and said, "It changes right there, in the middle of the page." "That's it!" McCleery agreed. "Up to that point, it's her usual work, competent, plodding, dull; then it suddenly becomes probing, imaginative, really interesting. But it's impossible that she would cheat. I know her too well to believe that." "Well," suggested Hollister, "why don't you invite her in? Say that you have a problem, that you trust her, but can't understand this break in the manuscript." "Why didn't I think of that. I'll do it."

The next day McCleery was back again, as excited as the day before. "I did what you suggested," he reported. "She broke down in tears. 'I had too much work,' she said. 'Couldn't finish on time. Finally, at I a.m., only halfway through, I decided just to put down my own ideas. I've never done it before. I know it isn't scholarly. But I didn't have time to finish another ten pages drawing entirely on the literature.' "

No matter what course titles we use, what structures we set up to conduct the courses, what combinations of courses we require for a degree, what calendar we schedule them into, the whole academic endeavor can come to grief if students misperceive what is meant by a liberal education and feel that they must comply with those misguided expectations. On the other hand, half the battle toward fulfillment is won if they either feel free to seek a liberalizing education out of their own choice or if they understand that the faculty will support them in doing so.

Many changes in higher education are made without a clearly thought-out linkage to a concept of liberal education. Change sometimes has utility apart from such a rationale. Change can oblige those who are set in their ways to re-do their plans, in the course of which they may at least freshen their work and, if they are so disposed, make other good changes. It can create good publicity, and many colleges could use a good press today. The publicity may be undeserved; nevertheless, it will serve the cause, however great or ignoble that may be. It can elicit a self-fulfilling prophecy that better things will happen, just because the students and faculty who are committed to the novelty believe that it will be good.

In seeking the path to college improvement, we might

as well capitalize upon these three tactics of institutional management if we can make them serve a truly worthy effort. Having acknowledged these insufficient reasons for change, however, we should look for better ones. I will do so by examining some currently notable ventures in higher education with the purpose of eliciting relevant principles for educational design. The ventures I will discuss are: contracted studies at Evergreen State College; the Bakan Plan; and project-oriented studies at Antioch College.

Contracted Studies

Evergreen State College of Washington opened in the fall of 1971 with a curriculum composed of coordinated studies and contracted studies. An individual or a small group may sign up with a faculty member to "earn credit by doing a specific project, carrying out a specific investigation, mastering a specific skill, or dealing with a specific body of subject matter." [1] This arrangement is called a contract to emphasize that it is "an agreement to do a piece of work and that it implies direct, mutual responsibility" between a student and the experienced person whom he has asked to help him.[2]

From discussion with the Evergreen faculty team attending this past summer's Danforth Workshop on Liberal Education, I understand that the rationale for offering contracted studies is complex. The option introduces flexibility into the curriculum. The planners expect great diversity of needs and interests among their students but limited resources in faculty and funds. The variety of coordinated studies (which are conceived as organized study activities involving some one hundred students and five faculty members for each "cooperative learning community") must be limited for efficiency's sake and for

[1] Evergreen State College, *Catalog,* 1970, p. 89.
[2] *Catalog,* p. 89.

pedagogical reasons; the complement of contracted studies permits student and staff initiative in supplementing the limited coordinated studies. Contracted studies is conceived as a vehicle for fostering the student's capacity for independent and continuing learning. This purpose is distinguished from "doing your own thing," which the Evergreen planners view as not requiring the sponsorship or guidance of a college at all. Contracted studies permits specialization that may not be possible within the available coordinated studies. This possibility is, of course, a part of the intended flexibility. The specialized or concentrated effort can be brief or long, intensive or not. Finally, contracted studies permits the combination of various strategies of inquiry: the use of work periods; travel; consultation with local or distant specialists; and so on. All of these concerns seemed to me, in conversations with Evergreen staff, to be integrated in the aim of engaging the motivation and energy of students while assuring their access to, and use of, professional experience and expertise.

The Evergreen Contracted Studies Program is just now coming into being, and it is hazardous to speculate about its effects. My impression is that these effects will be influenced in part by other factors that enter into the Evergreen context, such as the professionalism of the faculty, the allocation of faculty time to the contracted studies program, and the student mix.

Although faculty pedigrees are not shown in the *Catalog* and are played down in favor of an egalitarian ethos, the determination to elicit solid academic achievement in the terms of conventionally excellent liberal arts colleges shone through much of the talk I heard. There was in this talk a persistent concern with avoiding the captivity of traditional disciplinary majors; but the concern, in this sense, to foster interdisciplinary inquiry did not mean an unconcern about excellence of achievement within the timetable and types of measure typical of selective colleges. My experience is that faculty are rarely aware of the degree of constraint which their own unstated expectations exert upon students when the faculty have the instrument of a detailed contract as a means of enforcing expectations. In a large class a faculty member can rarely exert such influence. On the other hand, a faculty member who chooses to wink at language in the contract which means one thing to him and another to a student, or who is busy and preoccupied, or finds it distasteful to exercise close supervision may encourage "doing your own thing" even while deploring it. Thus the nature of faculty expectations and the extent to which faculty are authoritarian or authoritative in the instructional context will have more to do with what is learned than does the format of contracted as against coordinated studies. In terms of Sanford's types of professors, the effect of Evergreen's contracted studies will depend greatly upon the proportions of "stand pat academics," "radical accommodates to student values," and "integrates of new and old intellectual values."

One of the paradoxes about the recent surge of interest in tutorial and contracted studies is the fact that just at the time when faculty are showing a new willingness to enlarge these options, some students are reluctant to be bound by written contracts. This attitude is not necessarily in contradiction to their earlier message. It may be an expression of their suspicion that the faculty has figured out how, through the tutorial or contract format, to co-opt the students to do what the faculty wanted all along. A part of my experience with student-initiated seminars and tutorials is that students often misjudge at the beginning what they will later find relevant and sustaining. The failure to sustain effort is not always a result of irrelevance or unimportance in the contracted activity but may result from inexperience in managing time, conflict of a genuine interest with other crises in the life of the young person, the undertaking of too much interesting and important work, and so on. Thus students may be tempted to fall back upon external disciplines (grades, attendance requirements, syllabus demands) to keep them doing what they want to be kept doing. But it may also be the case that early discoveries in a seminar or tutorial or contract *ought* to be the occasion for revising the contract, and students are fearful that the instructor will be unwilling or reluctant to change at that point and that the contract will become a hindrance to the very flexibility it was meant to foster.

In response to this set of concerns, Antioch has tried some ventures in which a student's initial registration is entirely tentative and does not go on the registrar's record. In this case the faculty member is not responsible for keeping the student's nose to the grindstone, but only for being available, within limits agreed upon in advance, *if* the student completes work that warrants their meeting. When an endeavor is completed, the student submits to the faculty member a request for an award of credit, with a summary of work done and a statement as to what the student thinks was learned and what its significance was; the faculty member certifies the credit, if he agrees with the claim, and records his evaluation of the achievement. This pattern tends to produce a higher than normal proportion of unfinished courses: students claim and receive less than the normal amount of credits during the first term or two and then arrive with more than the average of completed projects by the third or fourth term, though still often with a lower aggregate of credits than the traditional schedule would yield. (Parents may be upset with this result, but Antioch typically judges the unrecorded learning as more than worth the missing credits.) This pattern does seem to have one of two effects: the student either leaves the college after a term or a year or becomes highly self-disciplined and productive, able to use either this open arrangement or a conventional one very efficiently.

Because of the fact that early and detailed clarity about expectations (including expectations about the option to revise expectations) can be so productive in learning, I favor a widely available option of contracted studies with clear and easy provisions for revision of contract. These studies should be staffed with faculty who are good listeners and imaginative in finding ways to enable both students and themselves to achieve through this method.

A contracted studies program can be so managed as to be either a costly or an economical use of faculty time relative to other instructional formats. Evergreen means the program to be efficient and, if I understand the staffing plans, has a very limited allocation of staff time to the program. There was also, in the Workshop, some nervousness about group meetings of students in contracted studies for fear that the distinction between the two formats would be lost. If student demand for contracted studies is low, and if student and faculty expectations about faculty role coincide, the results may prove happy for all parties. But if student demand is high, role expectations conflict, and students and faculty have different goals and standards as far as achievement within the program, the result could be counter-productive for both parties.

As a state university, Evergreen may be expected to attract a quite different mix of students from, for example, Oberlin College or even Wittenberg University. At the same time, the rhetoric of the Evergreen *Catalog,* dispersed in a section of the country with a sparse selection of private colleges, may attract a high proportion of students who would otherwise leave the state for more expensive options. The effects of a contracted studies program can be expected to be quite different in a protective-directive college (such as an unselective denominational school in George Stern's coding of College Characteristics Index and Activities Index scores),[3] collegiate-vocational culture on a typical state university campus, or an intellectual-expressive college such as Haverford, Antioch, or Reed.

From these considerations I infer that the following four factors are more important in the design of an "alternative

[3] G. G. Stern, *People in Context.* New York: Wiley, 1970.

academic pathway" than is the choice of faculty-drafted syllabus, student-initiated contract, or format of meetings among faculty and students for instruction: 1) process or relationship which elicits high student motivation is likely to improve the possibilities for learning; 2) insofar as student and faculty expectations as to faculty and student role are congruent, the possibilities for fruitful employment of student motivation and energy are improved; 3) the degree to which the types of learning sought by student and faculty member are clear and shared, or the degree to which the student and faculty member concur in clarifying and meeting one another's expectations on the achievement to be made will affect the efficiency as well as the types of learning significantly; 4) the degree of authoritarianism of faculty member and student will strongly affect the productivity of their relationship for learning. The last factor will also have substantial bearing upon the types of learning which can be facilitated by their relationship. Similarly, the combinations of faculty culture and student culture as discussed by Sanford will shape educational outcomes. (That is, different combinations will have different effects, and the merits of these effects may not coincide at all with one's views as to what constitutes maturity on the part of faculty or students.)

In stating these principles I do not mean to suggest that the contracted studies program is a worthless or misconceived venture. I mean rather that as faculty and academic administrators and students we should mold our expectations to what these principles suggest one can reasonably expect of such ventures. The factors at play in hindering or fostering learning are extremely complex, and our purpose in adopting a venture should be consonant with this reality. I believe that the format of contracts between students and faculty is a promising vehicle. Clarity at the beginning of a learning endeavor about expectations (as to roles, outcomes, procedures, style of participation) can greatly enhance its productivity, and the contract format facilitates that clarity if the parties are alert to its importance.

It is, however, only a vehicle, and it can be rendered worse than ineffective by either ignorance, indifference, or sabotage.

Bakan Plan

The Bakan Plan can be conceived as a contracted studies plan in which the professor writes a contract which prescribes at least three contact-hours per course in tutorial relationship as a requirement and may also prescribe readings, attendance of a lecture series, and other tasks. The contract may provide for student initiative in designing some of the tasks. The contract must also fit into certain institutional requirements such as utility in meeting distribution requirements, specification of prerequisites and a level of credit, and availability of syllabus for early announcement. As a group, professors offer enough options to permit students a significant choice of studies but few enough options to assure cost economy. (Bowen and Douglass have done an independent analysis of costs of this plan and find it, when further specified in certain ways, manageable at a reasonable cost by current standards.[4]) The Bakan Plan further provides that the student's permanent record contain, upon completion of a course, an attestation of satisfactory completion, with title and description of course, vita of professor, and statement of the student's assignments; failing completion, there is simply no record and no letter or numerical grade "or any form of evaluation or assessment of level of performance as in a conventional permanent record" is to be made.[5]

Bakan's purpose is to initiate educational reform in the direction of increased "freedom to teach" and "freedom to learn." The dynamic sought by the Bakan plan is one in which the teachers "teach that which they are competent to teach and

[4] H. R. Bowen and G. K. Douglass, *Cutting Instructional Costs.* Claremont, Calif.: Pomona College, Clarement University Center, 1970.

[5] D. Bakan, "A Plan for a College," *Canadian University and College,* June 1969.

that which they are interested in," students study what they are prepared and want to learn, and the integrity of the relationship between student and professor is protected, no matter how large the university. The plan is meant to encourage the student to become an independent learner and to proceed at his chosen pace. Institutionally-defined degree requirements keep the exercise of options by students and faculty within bounds viewed by the faculty as appropriate to the achievement of a liberal education. Insofar as the Bakan Plan is a form of contracted studies, the considerations already adduced apply also to it. Let me focus my analysis then upon two further features of the Bakan Plan: its attempt to link competence, freedom, and reasonable types and quantity of work for the faculty with good teaching; and its attempt to encourage quality education by "elimination of any permanent record of relative performance such as grades or even pass-fail."

The objective of linking competence in task to freedom in its choice and to reasonable work load is also shared by the Evergreen plans, but Evergreen has a different concept of the competence appropriate to the liberal arts faculty. The Evergreen faculty are expected, as their primary task in coordinated studies, to function as members of a small cooperative learning community and from their different backgrounds to bring their special experience to bear upon some of man's most urgent problems and his most highly prized values in a common effort to cut across the usual boundaries between academic disciplines. While the Evergreen faculty seem to me to conceive of their individual background competences in fairly conventional terms, they are expected as a community to grow new competence in tackling these interdisciplinary concerns. Such an objective is not precluded by the Bakan plan, but it lacks a process for fostering that objective. In a session with Evergreen faculty in the Danforth Workshop this past summer, considerable skepticism centered on the willingness of faculty to persist in gaining this new competence, on the market for them if they did so, and on the load involved in pursuing the effort. Whatever practice will eventually disclose about this skepticism, the Evergreen concept implies meanings of liberal education and faculty competence which differ from those of the more individualistic Bakan plan.

When Antioch attempted interdisciplinary integrating seminars for seniors in the late 1950s and early 1960s, there was a less tightly organized effort than Evergreen's to induce faculty collaboration in dealing with values and high priority social problems by interdisciplinary cooperation. A key difficulty was the reluctance of faculty to "teach something of which they were ignorant." And the faculty tended to define themselves as ignorant or competent much as Bakan would and much as I think Evergreen faculty are likely to do upon arrival. It is my own belief that a competent inquirer may actually be a more effective manager of learning in a group if he is not too far ahead of the group. In most courses the teacher is for the most part not a fresh inquirer. If he is, the subject of his inquiry is likely to be too advanced for the students or too esoteric for their interests or competence.

Not only are faculty likely to fear the task of Evergreen-type teaching, but they are unlikely to want to specialize in it. Some proportion of faculty can probably continue to be highly competent in both such teaching and a conventional discipline, but, I suspect, less than 20 per cent. If faculty are to want to sustain this particular competence, they must not only find the task itself rewarding but they must also be warranted in expecting professional rewards and status to accompany this choice of specialization. I favor the attempt to provide these conditions; providing them will require that many institutions cooperate in basing evaluation, compensation, and promotion upon the encouragement of such teaching, and disciplinary organizations must learn to prize this type of competence as one of their own priorities.

The Bakan plan contributes to our understanding that tutorial relationships can be enhanced by the use of lecture and other conventional resources and that extensive use of tutorials can be compatible with economical use of factulty. These arrangements also permit the distinction between being a "mother hen" and having a one-to-one student-faculty relationship which encourages mature independence and interdependence in intellectual inquiry. Tutorials have traditionally been excessively costly because they have involved too much tutor attention and even control of tutees by tutors. This same feature has often been educationally counterproductive because it produced, not collaborative and autonomous young scholars but imitators. If a student works less than twenty hours on his own between one tutorial session and the next, my own college can ill afford the tutorial. Moreover, if the student works less on his own, he is probably not making as rapid progress as he should be if he is an upperclassman.

My experience as an administrator of faculty load policies discourages me about efforts to define equity or to assign loads by the traditional formulae of numbers of courses, size of enrollments, diversity of preparations, numbers of contact hours, and so on. The very effort to manage in this way is increasingly costly and conceptually ridiculous the more elaborately one attempts to refine justice and control load. It is much better, if agreement can be reached to do so, to limit the proportion of full-time equivalent teachers to students, to agree on the desired types of relationship and work expected of faculty, and to leave it to the faculty, in groups of five to twenty, to decide among themselves what is equitable. Arbitration of serious problems is much less onerous and more likely to approximate equity in this framework than is the effort to audit elaborate load formulae. The less bureaucratic approach also seems to me more appropriate to the dignity of the faculty. Either the Evergreen or the Bakan plan can be administered in this spirit if the basic plan is taken as no more than a guideline to be approximated in the different faculty-student arrangements for study.

Bakan expects to achieve the needed integration of education through the modified laissez faire mechanism that faculty left to their choices will offer a diversity of things, that distribution requirements will force the student to use the opportunity, and that persuasion and self-interest will do the rest. He expects the use of prerequisites to take care of the need for that connectedness between courses that is required for students to have the proficiencies they need in a course (exams may be given to *admit* to courses where students do not have course credits that show proficiency). And Bakan challenges the presumption that professors know what a student should know and therefore ought to design his curriculum. All three of these considerations seem relevant to me, but they do not seem sufficient to insure the type of integration, either in particular courses or in the curriculum as a whole, that would characterize an adequate liberal education. In fact, however, I see no set of traps, hurdles, or Procrustean arrangements that can guarantee this desired result. Only if the commitments of faculty and of sufficient influential students favor the objective, and only if the teaching arrangements nurture the effort and compensate for human frailties with respect to the aim can we expect an adequate result. I suspect that the Bakan plan gives insufficient contextual support for this purpose.

I will not repeat here Bakan's reasons for doing away with grades or for regarding a pass-fail system as simply a two-valued grading system. I am generally in agreement with what he says on these points in his "A Plan for a College." Let me rather relate some recent experience on nongrading to the question of whether or under what conditions the abandonment of grades can serve the objective of a quality liberal education.

Antioch College abandoned grading of freshmen in 1965 and extended the no-grades policy to all students in 1968. As proposed by Bakan, no record is made of uncompleted work on the permanent record or transcript, though the counseling file contains a record of student and instructor comments on uncompleted work. In the spring of 1971 the college examiner surveyed senior reactions to the experience with this system. Forty per cent (in mid-February) indicated that they had applied to graduate study and an additional 40 per cent planned to apply. These figures compare with 61 per cent of the seniors of the preceding years; the percentage attending the next year is normally much lower than the percentage expecting eventually to do graduate work. Difference in aptitudes of students will contribute little if anything to this increase of graduate study expectations. A changing socio-economic mix of students may contribute (for example, students from lower income groups tend to have more upwardly mobile aspirations than other students), but it seems likely that the removal of stigmatization of mediocre or low grades may have released more students to aspire to graduate studies. This aspiration, however, may be a poor measure of quality of liberal education; it could even accompany a narrower professionalism than Antioch wants to foster.

Forty-three per cent of the Antioch respondents applying to graduate school reported that they had had "considerable" or "some" difficulty in explaining the meaning of their Antioch academic record to graduate schools, and of those yet to apply, 57 per cent expected to have difficulty. However, 75 per cent of the seniors were opposed to returning to grades in order to avoid the difficulties, preferring "the present system, but tightened up and enforced." One cannot extrapolate from the Antioch experience to other colleges in general because the college's reputation probably helped students get into graduate school who might otherwise not have succeeded. In addition, some students had used the cooperative plan (work-study) to do research or teaching assistant work at a university in whose graduate school they were interested, and had as a result letters of reference or personal contacts that facilitated their admission to graduate school.

Most important, 82 per cent of the seniors favored reforms in the system of reporting evaluations of student work. Contrary to the Bakan proposal, as I understand it, the students wanted an evaluative report which would serve potential employers and institutions in deciding whether to employ or admit the student and would assist the student in reassessing his own appropriate next vocational or educational moves. Seniors were very critical, in their free response comments, of faculty who wrote comments which amounted to grades ("excellent work," "an average student," "poor performance") or bore little relevance to appraisal of performance in relation to course objectives ("B didn't do well in this course, but he did better than I expected," or "makes for a congenial class," or "relates easily to others in the group"). What they wanted was a nonpunitive but analytic comment that would guide the student or a third party in understanding the student's capabilities and achievements.[6]

Again, it seems doubtful whether one can extrapolate from these students' comments to what a student population with different backgrounds and aspirations would say. On the other hand, I do infer that for students with above-average intellectual interests and with average to above-average ability, there may be less fear of professional appraisal in discursive terms related to learning objectives and vocational tasks than there is of two-valued, four-valued, or one hundred-valued grading scales. The coercion involved in grading systems and in external uses of them cannot be entirely eliminated if other modes of evaluation are reported, but it can be sufficiently attenuated that the benefits of competent appraisal seem to some students to outweigh the hazards. I would therefore regard it as a fundamental step in educational reform to eliminate the system-wide grading systems we have been using, but to encourage evaluative feedback, not only at the end of courses but

[6] L. Sparks and Churchill, R. "Antioch's Policy on Reporting Evaluations: A Survey of Graduating Seniors," Report #6, June 9, 1971.

throughout the instruction process. To link this point to the earlier one about the usefulness of clarifying and seeking congruency among student and faculty expectations, I would argue that periodic relating of performance to those expectations, with both peer and professorial perceptions as aids, can be another of the most productive elements of instructional strategy. If a student or group of students lacks the intellectual interests and motivations to withstand such feedback, then special effort ought to be given to eliciting and strengthening those interests and to developing the ego strength of students so that they can withstand criticism. Such a special effort may be particularly appropriate to fun-oriented campuses, for example, or to a campus that has predominantly low aptitude students or students with poor preparation for what faculty expect.

In closing my comment on the Evergreen Contracted Studies Program, I proposed four considerations that can help define an alternative academic pathway for a liberal arts college. Let me now add, as a derivative of the discussion of the Bakan Plan, the following considerations: 1) The extent to which students are actively exposed to competence among both peers and professors is a significant determinant of the learning they achieve, but the particular competences must be those which are to be learned, according to the college's objectives, if this benefit is expected to further those objectives. 2) The freedom to choose what and how one teaches or learns is probably positively related to level of motivation and thence to the productivity of instructional arrangements. Insofar as a college designs methods of achieving its degree objectives by means which permit greater than average freedom to choose the specific content and method of inquiry, it will probably get the benefit of this relationship. 3) The nature and intensity of faculty commitments as to work priorities are more important determinants of their effectiveness in meeting college purposes than are the mechanical features of policies on load, distribution requirements, and the like. At the same time, both program design and professional incentives should support the instructional purposes if these commitments are to work as they should. 4) Similarly, student priorities will shape the learning results in greater degree than will coercive features of grading, degree requirements, attendance policy, and the like; yet the desired commitments must be reinforced and enhanced by evaluative feedback that is supportive and diagnostically useful if the college's strategy for learning is to be efficient.

Project-Oriented Studies

The third and last particular venture which I will discuss here is the effort of the Washington-Baltimore Campus of Antioch to use a growing component of "project-oriented studies" as a vehicle of instruction. Evergreen plans to encourage students to engage in study or action projects both within the college and the larger community. Most colleges today give little more than lip service to the potential of work experience for higher learning, though more than 150 institutions now offer accreditable work opportunities for at least some of their students. Chickering has cited the widespread increase of options for students to experience first-hand the life and the world of which their books and professors speak and to try to integrate these two factors in understanding. Antioch is celebrating this year the fiftieth anniversary of its requirement that all students have substantial work and off-campus experience. For the past twenty years, at least, faculty and students have repeatedly complained that the relationship between what is found in books and professors and what is experienced on the job and away from campus is inadequately exploited for purposes of learning. Through all of these years we have tried, largely without significant success, to enhance this relationship. We have tried "sandwich courses" (with preplanning of how to use the job setting for learning). We have rewritten the cooperative syllabus, which spells out processes and content in the objectives for learning off campus and in the reporting and discussion of these matters with faculty and extramural advisers. We have tried "faculty in the field," faculty visiting the job from the home campus base, beefing up the teaching role of the job placement officers, and so on. These measures have largely seemed to have the effect of minor adjustments on a vehicle which is in general very potent but whose potency is little changed by minor adjustments. Wise heads would probably have given up on improving this endeavor, but we have kept trying. A recent product of the continued effort is a somewhat novel group of projects. Let me begin by describing three examples: the Middle Patuxent Valley Natural Inventory; the Rosewood State Training School Videotape; and the High School Equivalency Program of Colegio Jacinto Trevino.

The new town of Columbia, Maryland, is wrapped about several hundred acres of relatively undisturbed open space containing a segment of the valley of the Middle Patuxent River. Howard County farmers, ecology-minded students, and community-minded Columbians joined last year in forming an association to protect this valley and preserve it for recreational and educational uses. They urged the new town developer to make an immediate inventory of the bird and other animal life, plants, water quality, and topographical and historical features of the area in order that an intelligent approach might be taken to preserving as much as possible of the treasures of the area from the effects of the 120,000 population moving into the 15,000 acre town. After a look at the costs of a professional survey, the developer agreed to entrust the inventory to a citizen-college task force and provided $12,000 to do the job. With only two or three exceptions the students were unskilled and untrained. The citizens, however, included two of the country's most respected ornithologists, a hydrologist, a professional park naturalist, and a number of other biological and physical scientists in addition to professional urban planners. An Antioch faculty member—a biochemist—conducted a seminar in which a succession of these specialists took turns coaching the students on the methodology of specific types of field work and then accompanying them in the field until they were able to proceed with the survey. A project manager monitored the schedule of work performance. Wages were paid for the work hours but not for the study and seminar time. Some of the specialists received consultant fees; some who are active in the association declined pay. Cost to the developer was less than one-fourth that of a commercial survey of comparable scope and intensity.

Integrating the findings from the survey through the use of map overlays and field notes, the students identified and described distinctive subenvironments within the valley. In doing so, they found that the existing development plans would destroy certain unique and especially worthwhile environments, along with their patterns of bird, animal, and plant life. With the help of a student whose job was in the planning department of the developer, the task group went beyond its contract for inventorying the valley and proposed an alternative plan for developing the Cedar Lane South neighborhood. This student employee was able to demonstrate that the alternative plan would save investment capital, reduce operating costs of the public facilities (sewer, roads, and so on), house as many people as the earlier plans, and enhance the recreational resources of the area. He persuaded the company to adopt his plan. The citizens' association is now undertaking to persuade the county park authorities, the county zoning council, and the developer to proceed with development of a use plan for the valley as well as plans for drainage, sewer service, and zoning compatible with these educational and recreational uses.

The effect of the Middle Patuxent Valley Project in "turning on" students, eliciting disciplined work, and evoking clarification of their vocational and educational goals and continuity of self-managed effort has thus far been striking. The scientist who represented one of the citizen boards in appraising the project and who has participated professionally in such surveys characterized the report as superior to the usual commercial survey in its thoroughness, accuracy, and the caliber of probing the dynamics affecting the subenvironments studied. Clearly the interplay between work and study had an intimacy, an immediacy, and a relevance which are rare in Antioch experience. We have long had students who, for example, accomplished such facts as qualifying themselves on jobs with the National Labor Relations Board to answer questions in labor relations class that the professor could not answer; but the interplay of even these exceptional work opportunities with class work has generally been much less potent than in the project pattern.

In the Rosewood Videotape Project students who were working as attendants in a juvenile detention facility were permitted to videotape thirty hours of interviews with inmates and staff as illustration of the conditions and attitudes in the Home. The raw tape was edited into a 2½ hour report which eventually found its way to both the state authorities controlling juvenile homes and the court officers who sentence youth to terms in such homes. The effect was prompt and startling. It was the more startling because earlier written reports from more professional sources had languished in the files.

The high school equivalency program of Colegio Jacinto Trevino is closer in design to normal practicum or internship arrangements. A group of graduate students in teacher education who are themselves Mexican-American undertook as their practicum to assist some fifty high school dropouts ranging in age from seventeen to over forty to complete high school and take equivalency examinations. The graduate students' participation earns grant support for their program and thus makes the economics of their own education manageable.

The seminar activity integral to these projects is, of course, interdisciplinary, but it differs significantly from much that goes by the name "interdisciplinary studies." It is easy for such studies to be so abstract as to lose clear meaning or so superficial as to come off as either tautology or falsehood. The cry for "value-oriented studies," which often characterizes the effort to do interdisciplinary work as an integral demand of liberal education, leads all too easily to sermonizing. Or, in the name of objectivity, the teacher treats issues of worth, right, and justice in a wishy-washy way. The concreteness of the problems tackled in these projects and the specificity of the conditions with which the students had to cope were insurance against meaningless abstraction. The importance of the problems to the people affected and the linkage of student work with accountability for their wages are a help in driving out superficiality. In the region of Colegio Jacinto Trevino, for instance, almost 80 per cent of Chicano children drop out before the end of high school, and the project leaders attribute this excessive rate (compared to dropout rates of Caucasians in the area) to bias in the schools against the use of Spanish, the abilities of Spanish-speaking children, and the ways and values of Mexican-American culture. In each of the projects there was a great amount of disagreement about what was good or best to do, but in each case it was necessary to act. Intellectual disagreement and suspension of judgment were open to individuals, but action upon some collective judgment representing such agreement as could be reached served to force the group to eschew detached lecturing or refusal to decide.

In projects of the type here cited, there is a specific fact situation which has to be understood in order for a worthwhile effort to be carried out. This condition sets up an ideal motivation for rigor in data gathering, in analysis of alternative options for action, and in argument as to reasons (theory) for what is proposed and done. These examples suggest a further set of considerations useful in designing alternative pathways in liberal education: 1) A learning endeavor in which the teacher's and the learner's primary ethical concerns gain expression is likely to activate greater motivation than one in which curiosity alone is the primary drive. 2) Strategies of learning which engage students with significant work and with genuine problems of high social priority are more likely to enable them to connect theory with practice, idea with referent, and word with meaning than strategies which rely on books and abstractions alone. Thus the interplay of work and study, experience and abstraction is likely to yield greater rigor in methodology of inquiry, both in data gathering and interpretation and in the examination of competing ideas, than is a methodology that foregoes this interplay. 3) A learning strategy which engages community talent with that of the college is likely to enrich the pool of competence beyond that otherwise available to the college.

How are the eleven principles here mentioned related to what is said elsewhere in this book about improved educational technology, current faculty cultures, and trends in social change? If the processes and tools of instructional technology merely increase instructors' control over students or facilitate students' self-subjugation to what they fancy others want, the result will be counterproductive. It will be a mix of greater mastery of externally dictated tasks with a loss of self-mastery, or critical judgment and imaginative capability. North equates individualization with more precise tailoring of externally dictated processes on externally directed tasks by the use of improved tools. The individualization that requires student choice of objectives or student invention of processes or tools is omitted and ignored. This is not to say that instructors should dictate no tasks or that students should choose their processes and tools at will. In 1957–1961, an Antioch experiment in diverse independent study strategies made substantial use of coaching by programed or semi-programed methods within a framework of instructor-selected objectives. Moreover, pre- and post-testing permitted impact measures. The objectives, however, usually included a provision for student input or substitutions among the objectives and for processes and tools that defy present skills in statistically precise measurements of impact. It would be sad, indeed, if educators confuse accountability on their mandate with reporting gains on subordinate or low priority goals at the cost of losses on, or neglect, of, more difficult and higher priority goals such as the types of competence, autonomy, understanding, and integrity discussed by Chickering.

The systems discussed by North are still only subsystems of the alternative academic pathways which we should be offering as college degree programs. These pathways should be much more nearly comprehensive designs, strategies, and frameworks for complex, integrated, though open (that is, ever revised) purposes.

Epilogue

I opened this essay with the story of a student who for years had done what she thought the professors wanted instead of expressing her own ideas, which the teachers found both more interesting and intellectually more valuable. I have closed with three stories of students who became engaged in vital tasks in the local community, the accomplishment of which required them to improve their methods of study and to add to their grasp of theory and fact. In all of this discussion, we have been seeking some guidelines as to how to design the pathways of liberal learning in order to provide it best. No one of the pathways discussed has been given a full analysis, and the guidelines stated are simply examples of what might go into a more adequate definition of the criteria for an adequate program of liberal education.

The pathways most needed in liberal education today are not simply good segments of the academic way, but comprehensive alternatives that facilitate a student's achieving what a college education should mean, what a liberal education ought to be and do. I have presupposed throughout a point of view on this topic: that a liberal education gives priority to cultivating the student's intellect; developing his capacity for independent judgment and critical thought; freeing him to appreciate or to differ from some of the limitations of his family background, peer culture, and other environmental influences; enabling him to develop an integrated view of his world and of himself; and thus to take leadership in serving both his own development and that of his society better than he otherwise might. Because these terms are at once abstract and ambiguous when offered only in such words, I have sought to illustrate the purpose of liberal education with more concrete attempts to achieve that purpose. It now remains to ask: What other considerations should enter into the design of our academic pathways if they are to fulfill these complex aims of a liberal education appropriately for our circumstances? And without awaiting a full reply, we should be at work testing the pathways that seem promising with the meager understanding that we do have now.

Chapter 6

Technology Rewards Its Teachers

R. Stafford North

There are shortages in all areas of education today but one. Education has plenty of critics. Parents and legislators say it is too expensive; student protestors say it is irrelevant and ineffective; teachers say that it pays too little and demands too much; and observers from nearly every quarter say it is too rigid and inflexible. Two of the most constructive critics of education today are Peter Drucker and Sidney Tickton. In *The Age of Discontinuity,* Drucker states:

> *There is a great need for a new approach, new methods, and new tools in teaching, man's oldest and most reac-*

tionary craft. There is great need for methods that will make the teacher effective and multiply his or her efforts and competence. Teaching is, in fact, the only traditional craft in which we have not yet fashioned the tools that make an ordinary person capable of superior performance. In this respect, teaching is far behind medicine, where the tools first became available a century or more ago. It is, of course, infinitely behind the mechanical crafts where we have had effective apprenticeship for thousands and thousands of years.[1]

Drucker further suggests two crises that will force education to change whether or not educators may wish it: the economic crisis facing education due to low productivity (there will not be enough people to do the job even if there were the money to pay them) and the pedagogic crisis indicated by both the lack of learning in schools and the current rebellions.[2]

Sidney Tickton, of the Academy for Educational Development, edited the recently published *Report by the Commission on Instructional Technology* to the Congress and the President. In this report, Tickton and the Commission suggest, "Dissatisfaction with American education is everywhere evident. Opinions as to what should be done often contradict each other. But there is a clear demand for action that will enhance the learning of the individual student, the effectiveness of schools and colleges, and ultimately the quality of the nation's life." The *Report* discloses three significant conditions which characterize education today:

Impeded education: Learning in American schools and colleges is impeded by such troubles as the increasing gap between education's income and needs, and shortages of good teachers in the right places.

Unresponsive education: The organization of schools

[1] P. Drucker, *The Age of Discontinuity* (New York: Harper and Row, 1968), p. 26.

[2] Drucker, pp. 334–336.

and colleges takes little account of even what is now known about the process of human learning, including the range of individual differences among learners and styles of learning. This condition makes schools particularly unresponsive to the needs of disadvantaged and minority-group students.

Outmoded education: The ways that students learn outside school differ radically from the ways they learn inside school. Formal education makes only limited use of the many means of communication which society at large finds indispensable.[3]

It might be easy to conclude from these comments that there is nothing right about American education, but that would be decidedly unfair. After all, the present system produces more than twice the number of college graduates per 100,000 population than any European nation.[4] We have made great demands of our educational system—both in quantity and in quality—and some remarkable achievements have resulted. We clearly are facing, however, a situation in which "business as usual" will not do—neither for the present nor the future. Just as modern society has given education some problems to solve, however, modern society has also given education the means for solving them. One of the truly promising possibilities on the horizon for education today is instructional technology. This was, indeed, the conclusion of the Commission on Instructional Technology already mentioned: "The multiple problems that confront American education have no single solution. But learning could be significantly improved if the technology and techniques of the so-called second industrial revolution—the revolution of information processing and communication—could be harnessed to the tasks of the schools and colleges." [5]

[3] S. G. Tickton (Ed.), *To Improve Learning. Vol. 1. An Evaluation of Instructional Technology* (New York: Bowker, 1970), p. 16.

[4] *UNESCO Statistical Yearbook* (Paris: UNESCO, 1969), pp. 265, 269–273.

[5] Tickton, p. 19.

Let us examine, then, just what this instructional technology can do for education generally and for liberal arts colleges particularly.

Instructional Technology and Educational Improvement

The less-used but more significant definition of instructional technology considers it as "process." According to this view, technology, as applied to education, can provide a much-needed system or overall design for instruction. This "systems approach" states a specific, measurable outcome in terms of student behavior and then marshalls all available instructional resources toward the achievment of this objective. The strength of instructional technology in this sense is not that it provides an entirely new set of elements for education, but rather that it puts the same basic ingredients into a sharper focus and makes them work together more effectively and efficiently. One of the essentials of viewing technology as a system is the use of the management technique of modeling to demonstrate visually the desired educational outcome and the contribution each element in the instructional process can make toward achieving this outcome. One way of modeling the most basic aspects of instruction, for example, is shown in Figure 1.

In this model, "terminal behavior" indicates the instructional objective—a description of student performance or behavior. This statement of the terminal behavior may describe either concrete skills or abstract values, but it is always given in terms of measurable, observable actions which the student can perform to demonstrate his achievement of the desired objective. One terminal behavior, for example, might state, "The student can read material on the level of the *Reader's Digest* at five hundred words per minute with 90 per cent comprehension." Another might suggest, "The student can demonstrate his ability to appreciate poetry by identifying 80 per cent of the figures of speech and allusions in thirty lines of poetry." The key to the process of learning through instruc-

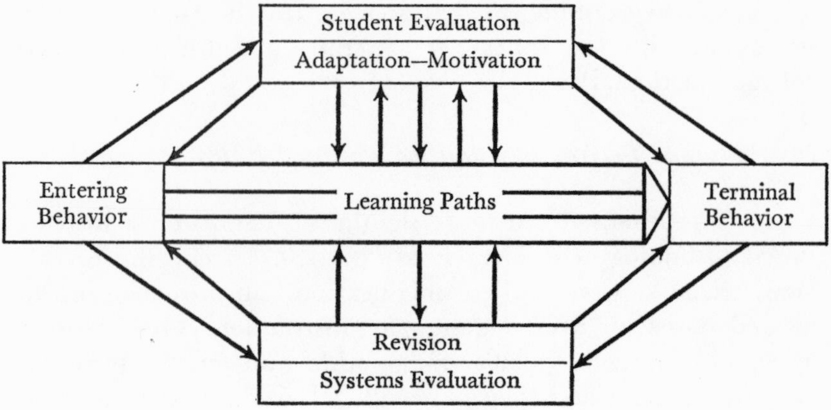

Figure 1

tional technology is this statement of objectives because it permits a relatively exact measurement of accomplishment. Such objectives describe student achievement, not teacher activity or subject matter. An objective, for example, which states "The course will cover each instrument in a symphony orchestra" does not provide a measurable outcome in student performance which can serve as a basis for building the instructional system. Rather, the objective should indicate, "The student can identify each instrument in a symphony orchestra from its sound" or "can place each instrument into its correct category of instruments."

On the opposite side of the model is "entering behavior," which refers to the student's status on the terminal behavior at the time he enters the program. If a student can already perform the terminal behavior when he begins, for example, there is little point in making him proceed through every step. If, on the other hand, a student is so far from the objective that regular procedures or the usual time allotment will not enable him to reach the objective, it is much better to know this from the beginning and adjust accordingly. The failure to obtain and utilize information about entry behavior is one of the greatest weaknesses of college programs. We all know, for instance, that students who enter a college class in chemistry, speech, composition, or history have widely differing backgrounds and capacities. With only a few exceptions, however, we give all these students the same learning plan, the same length of time in which to complete it, and then expect them to be at about the same point by the final exam.

The next item on the model is obvious. We must develop some means for taking the student from his entry point to where we believe he should be in the terminal behavior. These means, or "learning paths," may be anything from lectures and group discussion to independent study and work experiences. Simulation, readings, audio or video tapes, projects, field trips, films—any of these and many other approaches may be included in a teacher's repertoire of learning paths. In a fully developed system, indeed, there should be more than one learning path available by which a student may reach any terminal behavior. This allows the student an alternative path if the first does not appear to suit his needs or interests.

In the upper box on the model is "student evaluation." Evaluation supplies information on each student's entering behavior, his progress as he moves down the learning paths, and his attempts to demonstrate the terminal behavior. Evaluation, then, is more or less constant—providing the teacher with continual feedback on the student's status, progress, and problems. Since students will be progressing at a variety of rates, this evaluation must be individualized enough that the instructor knows the progress of each student and not just the class average. On the basis of this evaluation, the instructor can treat students who are in the learning paths in the appropriate manner. Some may not be making progress because they cannot learn well on the path they are using or because they have exhausted the material available in that mode without having reached the terminal behavior. In this case, the teacher must adapt the program to the needs of the student. Perhaps a student needs to be shifted to a different learning path or needs to be "branched" through additional segments of instruction or given special counseling. The role of the teacher includes directing this adaptation to individual needs.

Others may be failing to make progress not because they have found some learning program inadequate but because they either have not used a learning program or have not used it well. They are not sufficiently stimulated to learn and need some type of motivation—perhaps a better understanding of the values of reaching the given objective or some extrinsic reward. Both adaptation and motivation are based on student evaluation and can be used effectively only when the evaluation is adequate.

The lower box completes the system by giving it a built-in means for improvement. Information on students also flows to "systems evaluation." How many students, for example, reached the objective and in what length of time? How many reached the objective through one learning path and how many through another? How does the time spent to reach the objective compare between paths? What do before and after tests show on the amount of change? How does the cost and effectiveness of one learning path compare with another? On the basis of such information, the system can be revised.

In one sense, of course, none of the elements on this model is new. For centuries teachers have used objectives, evaluation, motivation, learning paths, and program revision. Instructional technology, however, has suggested that the objectives be stated in exact, measureable standards of performance and that all other aspects of the system be organized to contribute toward helping the student reach these standards. This design or process is, then, the first major contribution of instructional technology to education.

The second and more familiar definition of instructional technology recognized by the Commission considers instructional technology to be "the media born of the communications revolution which can be used for instructional purposes alongside the teacher, textbook, and blackboard."[6] In this sense, technology deals with instructional media or, in terms of the model, with learning paths. While the first view of instructional technology provides process, this view provides tools.

Generally the new tools are well-known—television; programed instruction; computer-assisted instruction; audio recordings; more versatile projectors; dial access systems to information; miniaturization through microforms, simulations, and many others. While a detailed view of any of these is unnecessary here, an important observation on the relationship between the two definitions of instructional technology should be made: the new tools and the new process are somewhat dependent on each other. As long as the teacher must serve as the primary source of information and as long as most of the instructional process must be built around a teacher working with students in relatively large groups, we are not likely to make much progress toward the improvement of instruction. Many of the new tools, however, allow students to work separately—or in small interacting groups—at a rate and through a means suited to their own needs. As the student becomes less directly dependent upon the teacher for information, the teacher can take on a broader role of managing the instructional program rather than serving simply as dispenser of information.

The Commission found that, by and large, the use of the new instructional tools which technology has provided has not yet been particularly successful. This is due at least in part to the fact that the new tools have simply been added to the program without utilizing the new process.[7] Long ago, Jesus explained the futility of putting new wine into old wineskins; the same applies to instructional technology. Only when we use the new tools and the new process together will we make the changes required to meet the challenge in education today.

[6] Tickton, p. 21.
[7] Tickton, p. 13.

Results of Utilizing Instructional Technology

Instructional technology makes possible better adaptation to individual needs. At Oklahoma Christian College, for example, we have developed a freshman composition course around the systems model. The desired level of writing skill is stated in performance terms and students are tested at the point of entry to determine how near to the goals they are. Adaptation to individual needs first enters the picture here, for those who demonstrate achievement of the objectives are given credit and allowed to move on to other work. For those who do not pass initially, the pre-test serves as diagnosis. After each student's needs are analyzed, a program is developed which will enable him to reach these goals. Since not all needs are alike, not all programs are alike. Some students listen to tape recordings on paragraphing or punctuation; others write exercises on agreement of subject and verb. Each student writes a paper each week and reviews the paper with a senior English major who serves as his tutor throughout the program. As soon as the tutor believes the student is ready to demonstrate achievement of the final objectives, he may attempt the final writing exam. Whenever he demonstrates the required level of achievement, he is through with the course and receives credit. If, by the end of the trimester he is still unable to write as well as required, he simply receives a "withdrawn" in the course and re-enrolls for the following term. This allows him still more time without giving him an "F" to overcome, and he is not expected to repeat the material he already knows. (The re-enrollment allows the college to receive additional funds since he is costing more to get through the program.) Such adaptation to individual needs can enable education to meet some of its most pressing problems—providing for disadvantaged and minority groups, allowing the advanced student to move rapidly so that he does not lose interest, and becoming more efficient through allowing students to work on their specific needs rather than putting each student through exactly the same program.

Instructional technology also improves learning. Exact results are difficult to obtain because absolute connections between cause and effect in learning are difficult to establish. We all know that most studies of the newer media show no significant difference in the amount of learning. There are some notable exceptions, however. Students who take the composition program described above, for example, are more likely to pass the English proficiency test at OCC than are their counterparts who have not. The teachers involved in the program agree that their students write better after this one-hour course than they previously did after the first three-hour composition course. Jasper, working with the Navy training program, found that through revision of certain films 98 per cent of the students reached program objectives in one-sixth the original time.[8] Postlethwait converted his Purdue botany course to utilize both the process and the tools of technology. He reports that "grades, for example, have improved, efficiency in space and equipment utilization has risen significantly, staff effort has been directed to specific student needs, and it has been possible to cover more subject matter in far less time."[9] Such gains are difficult to produce and require time for development and revision. There is a growing amount of evidence to suggest, however, that instructional technology can, indeed, achieve such improvements.[10]

Instructional technology also can provide greater productivity. As suggested earlier, productivity is one of the major problems to which education must address itself. We must

[8] L. C. Twyford, Jr., "Educational Communications Media," in *Encyclopedia of Educational Research* (4th ed.) (London: Collier-Macmillan, 1969), p. 370.

[9] S. N. Postlethwait, "Time for Minicourses?" *Library-College Journal,* Winter 1969, *2,* 25.

[10] Twyford, pp. 367–380.

find ways of getting more for each dollar and we must find ways of making more efficient use of manpower. The Commission's *Report* suggests that new approaches do have something to offer in this area and cites the Navy's Memphis Air Training Center at which twenty-five courses utilizing programed instruction reduce training time by 28 per cent. In a single year, 235 man years of student and teacher time were saved.[11] Again referring to our composition program at OCC, the cost is about three times less than the traditional method.[12]

Technology will not replace the teacher, but it can make some useful changes in the teacher's role by decreasing the time spent in routine chores and increasing the time spent directly with pupils and dealing with them in uniquely human ways. This kind of productivity will, in some instances, reduce the overall cost of education, while in other cases it will increase the total educational output so that we can make greater achievements without corresponding increases in costs. Of course, equipment and material development expense are sometimes great enough to offset any actual savings for a long period.

Finally, instructional technology provides a sound basis for accountability—perhaps the most discussed concept in education today. As costs rise, as education is subjected to closer scrutiny and its inadequacies become apparent, as enthusiastic claims are made for new methods, accountability becomes more important. It is the theme of many current educational conferences and the issue in many negotiations and policy decisions.

Instructional technology is the means by which we can assess accountability. The only true basis for cost-effectiveness figures is a measure of learning output; the best basis available for determining learning output is measureable objectives; and

[11] Tickton, p. 32.

[12] S. G. Tickton, *Summary Report of an Evaluation of the Learning Center and Related Programs at Oklahoma Christian College* (Oklahoma City: Oklahoma Christian College, 1970), p. 25.

the system for developing and achieving measureable objectives is the process of instructional technology. In the end, the greatest contribution of technology to education may be the clarification of objectives and the accurate measurement of how well these objectives are achieved. In this way we can then indicate with some assurance just how many students are achieving specified goals and can seek more funds, offer merit pay to teachers, or determine which "hardware" or "softwear" to buy because of its proved outcome. Accountability can be achieved in direct proportion to the extent to which the process of technology is applied to instruction.

Technology Applied to the Liberal Arts College

Those familiar with the conditions of private liberal arts colleges today will not have missed the implications of instructional technology for such colleges. The small-college claim to give individual attention, for instance, can no longer be based simply on a low student-faculty ratio. Rather, adaptation to individual student needs will become a function of the wise use of technology. When used to meet individual needs as part of a carefully designed system, instructional technology becomes a means of increasing rather than decreasing humanization. If liberal arts colleges wish to sell themselves as offering individual attention, then they will need to incorporate the adaptation instructional technology makes possible.

Liberal arts colleges have also emphasized superior instruction. As more technology is developed and applied, those institutions properly employing it will achieve the highest quality in learning. Technology also offers the liberal arts college an opportunity to improve productivity. While not every application of technology to instruction results in reduced costs, ample evidence indicates that such efficiency can be obtained.

With liberal arts colleges, along with other institutions,

being asked to justify their existence, their effectiveness, and their expenditures, the opportunities technology affords for demonstrating results should not be overlooked. These colleges must be accountable, and such accountability can best be achieved through the exact approach to instruction which technology makes possible.

As many have pointed out, of course, there are problems and obstacles in the use of technology in education. Although not all the tools are new to us, their implementation requires adjustments, training of faculty, development of materials, and investment in equipment. If they, like other tools, are used carelessly the results can be harmful. In spite of these problems, however, instructional technology is more than just a fad. There is real substance in the prospects it offers, and of all the segments of our educational system, none stands to profit more than the private college. Instructional technology alone is not likely to save a college; it might not be an overstatement, however, to suggest that few, if any, private colleges will long continue which ignore or reject it completely.

We are living at a great time in the history of education. The challenge is magnificent and the opportunities exciting. When Valvert encountered Cyrano de Bergerac in the theatre, he said to him, "Your nose is rather large." Cyrano was aghast but not because someone had accused him of having a sizable nose, for that was obvious. Rather he was amazed that with all the possibilities his nose presented, Valvert could think to say only, "Your nose is rather large." Education too has almost unlimited possibilities; unlike Valvert, let us make the most of them.

Chapter 7

Learning Environments

Conrad Hilberry

A week ago yesterday, my wife and I left the black-topped road near Jackson in Breathitt County, Kentucky. For about twenty miles we followed a gravel road along Quicksand Creek, a road that had been widened so that trucks could haul coal out from the strip mines. The trucks came heavy and fast; sometimes the dust was so thick we had to slow almost to a stop to keep from running off the road. The person who had given us directions said we should turn off sharp to the right just before we got to the bottom of the second mountain—we couldn't miss it. He was right; there was no sign, but only one road turned off on that side of the mountain. No trucks now. We followed this dirt road around another mountain for four or five miles to Decoy. Located at a fork in Quicksand Creek, Decoy can hardly be called a community. There is a post office, a store, and the Decoy school. The twenty-five or so families that have a Decoy mailing address are scattered up and down the branches of Quicksand Creek, seldom in sight of each other. Their children come in from as far as three miles to the Decoy school.

If we are talking about learning environments, this is not a promising one, however much one's romantic impulses may be stirred by the beauty and isolation of the mountains. Few of the parents are much impressed with the need for education; if it is raining or if there is wood to be chopped, that is reason enough for keeping the children out of school. Few of the children have seen any part of the country but their own or any city larger than Hazard or Jackson. There is little hunting or fishing in the mountains anymore and the hills are too steep to farm. If the men work, it is "on the strip job" or for a logging company; most of the families live on welfare or pensions. Yet Decoy has been a remarkably effective elementary school for twenty or thirty years. The eighth graders have gone on to the county high school at Hindman, which means boarding during the week at the Hindman Settlement School. A remarkable number of the high school graduates have gone on to college, usually at Berea or Lee Junior College in Jackson, or Morehead State. Lionel and Frankie Duff, the teachers at Decoy school, boast that no student who has finished eighth grade at Decoy is on welfare.

We are hoping in the next couple of months to find out a good deal more than we now know about the learning environment—so to call it—at Decoy. What is there about Decoy school that can move students out of lethargy into a lively interest in the world? The answer, of course, is that the Duffs are extraordinary teachers. But more specifically, how do they do it? The day that we were there, we didn't see any of the razzle-dazzle techniques you read about—no fancy mathematical games that teach the students calculus without their knowing what has happened to them. Most of the time, the students worked away in workbooks, grades one through four in one room, grades five through eight in another, generally fairly quiet whether one of the Duffs happened to be in the room or not. They worked in clusters of two or three, the older children sometimes helping the younger, the teachers going from one group to another, explaining things. The older kids had a spelling bee and the younger ones half listened. Nothing sensational. Just two skilled teachers keeping eight grades going, doing janitorial work, transporting children to and from school in their carry-all, supervising a part-time cook who prepared hot breakfast and lunch for the children. It must be much like the one-room grade school that my mother attended near here in Niota, Illinois, and that rural children attended all over the country before busing and consolidation.

But as we thought about it afterwards, we remembered some incidents and artifacts that were unobtrusively there, in the background. When we first arrived, for example, Lionel Duff took a good deal of time to explain to us the genealogical chart on the bulletin board just inside the door of his classroom. While the children were going about their work—or wondering who we might be—he traced back the ancestry of some of the children in the room as far as seven generations to the first settlers in that hollow. His wife, Frankie, grew up in Decoy and is herself related to the earliest settlers and to many, possibly all, of the children. Near the genealogical chart were a number of photographs, one of Seattie Smith, a formidable-looking woman, great grandmother to several of the children. The photograph showed her with only one leg. The other had been amputated in Lexington, Lionel told us. Her family built a boat and took her a two-day journey down the creek to the road to get her to the hospital. While we were talking, Woodrow, one of the students, was up on a ladder putting some pictures on the wall. When we asked, he pointed out some of his own pictures. His specialty, apparently, was cows—often with enormous udders and as many as six or seven teats. Woodrow had a feeling for cows and was clear about his connection with them. Actually, the art work seemed to us striking, and it turned out that some Decoy pictures had been shown in a children's exhibit at the Metropolitan Museum a few years back. One of them had won a prize. Later, Lionel told the students one of the Jack stories, a folk tale, embellishing it freely and setting it in a place much like Decoy.

The genealogies, the pictures, Lionel Duff's stories of Seattie Smith and Jack all tell the students, who might otherwise have considered themselves backward and dull, that they belong to a place where funny, treacherous, and heroic things have happened. They are part of a saga. At Decoy, the learning environment was notable not for an unusual curriculum nor a stimulating mixture of students, nor for its architecture, cultural opportunities, nor the variety and motion of a city. It was notable for pictures, charts, stories—for the teachers' steady conviction that those students come from an important place and people and that they can do work that might be praised in New York City.

I have mentioned Decoy partly as a caveat to remind us that "environment" is subtle. With the same building, the same curriculum, the same students, the same rules, but with different teachers, Decoy could easily have become a place where students learned to despise themselves or, if they were too healthy for that, to despise school. With that warning, let me turn to colleges and to talk about curriculum, architecture, and some of the other less subtle, more manageable matters that may or may not turn out to be important.

The 1960s appear in retrospect to be the decade of "the great pulling apart" in American colleges. It seems to me that one can identify at least three impulses that have pulled student allegiance away from the campus. The three impulses drive in quite different directions; they may sometimes rest on naïve or romantic assumptions but each implies a criticism of the college as a learning environment. The first of these impulses is a back-to-the-world movement. Virtually every college felt the pressure of this impulse during the sixties, and many colleges accommodated themselves by significant changes in program. It is no longer just Antioch or Northeastern or Cincinnati or Kalamazoo or the Associated Colleges of the Midwest that send students off to jobs in Boston or Washington or Santa Fe or out of the country for study, research, or the experience of living with a family in Algiers or Kyoto or Beirut. As nearly as I can make out, every college has some sort of Appalachian term or internship in a medical mission in Korea or apprenticeship to a sculptor in New York City or January survival course in the Monongahela National Forest.

This drive away from the campus to jobs, to unfamiliar cultures, or to situations that promise more intense learning than the campus can provide—this drive seems to me the most significant change to overtake the colleges in the 1960s, deeper and more permanent in its effects than the celebrated surge of political activity during that decade. How are we to account for this longing to be elsewhere? Partly, of course, the explanation is that these off-campus experiences *are* magnificent opportunities for learning. We have known all along, I guess, that apprenticeship was one excellent way to learn a trade or an art and that exposure to an alien culture in one's own country or abroad could make one vividly aware of his own habits and attitudes—even his own gestures or his sense of time and space. It just took us an unconscionable length of time to follow Antioch's example and put this knowledge to work.

The explanation may also be, partly, that the students now in college, especially in the somewhat selective colleges, have been going to school too long and too intensively. Many of them have never held full-time jobs except perhaps at a summer camp, and some of them have never held part-time jobs except delivering papers, let's say, or babysitting. Since they were three or four, they have been going to school, usually under some pressure. No wonder they would rather be slapping tortillas in a Mexican village. Where this is not true, where schooling has been interlarded with regular jobs, that impulse to get off campus is much less pronounced. At Friends University in Wichita, for example, students showed little enthusiasm for a co-op program that promised to place them in jobs. Why all the excitement about a job? The great majority of them worked already, as much as thirty hours a week. They have always had some kind of job. I believe this was Wilberforce's experience, too, when its co-op program was first introduced. A co-op program can do a great deal, of course, even at schools like these, but students do not rush to the employment office. One can think of other explanations as well. Our students, like all participants in the counter-culture, put a high value on experience of any kind, pleasant or painful, so long as it is intense. They lament the flatness of standard American lives. Nothing happens. We are too insulated by houses, cars, clothes, social roles, and insurance policies for any real experience to get through to us. Some of them, I dare say, see college as another sort of insulation. They would rather be miserable fighting mosquitoes in Malawe than suffer a mild ennui on campus.

But sooner or later we have to mention the possibility that our campuses may not be particularly inviting places. Actually, I myself am addicted to campuses; I can't seem to leave them alone. But it is true that the academic part of a campus—I mean the classroom—is invariably the least attractive. There are almost never any bookshelves there nor anything to read, seldom any picture on the wall or any comfortable furniture. It never occurs to one that he might sit around and talk or read after a class if the room is not being used. Except for an occasional room that was intended to be something else, our classrooms have no character. They are as indistinguishable as development houses. For a large course at Kalamazoo our audio-visual people projected pictures on the walls and played music while we were entering the room before class. It did a lot for the tone of the whole enterprise. Even a big poster of a distinguished poet—let's say W. C. Fields—would add style to a classroom.

But if our campuses are less inviting than they should be, it is not primarily because of the architecture. Or, rather, the architecture is a symptom of another disease. The Georgian brick repetition must go deeper than the buildings. It is frighteningly easy for faculty members and colleges to become repetitive or conventional or self-protective. If this is entropy, it is a powerful principle. Liveliness in teaching and learning requires an endless series of fresh starts and happy accidents; even this year's discovery will not be a discovery next year. Well, it may still glow pretty convincingly next year, but the year after that it is part of the routine. The students' discovery that they can learn very successfully in other settings besides the campus has been an exhilarating fresh start. It may provoke us to make some fresh starts of a related kind closer to home (more about this possibility later).

The second impulse pulls in the opposite direction. It is the impulse to scrutinize oneself, often in the magnifying mirror of intense personal relationships. If the first impulse scattered students, during the 1960s, into jobs and homes and studies all over the world, the second drew them into the tight and self-regarding circle of communes. If the first was an attempt to get closer to the lives of a variety of people in their own habitats, the second is an attempt to create a special community, deliberately unlike the superculture that washes over all of us, an alternative style of life. This impulse may seem the unkindest cut of all to the private colleges. Typically, they have prided themselves on being residential—communities of learners, places where students make lifelong friendships. Now it appears that relationships among students even at small colleges are made formal or impersonal by room assignments, dormitory corridors, rules governing when one must be in or simply the requirement that one must live on campus. Students are insisting on the right to become fully aware of their own preferences, inhibitions, and convictions by experimenting freely with the organization of their own social lives. A Kalamazoo graduate, now living in a commune, asked "Why should

I be creative only with a canvas or a pen when I could be creative with my life?" This is an impulse not only to determine one's life but to participate fully in it—to do one's own work. A Kansas State student remembers clearly the occasion when she realized, living in a dormitory, that she was not buying or cooking her own food, nor keeping herself warm, nor washing her dishes or clothes, nor cleaning up after herself. Everything she needed appeared in front of her and someone came in discreetly and removed all her debris. It seemed to her that she was living at second hand. Surely not all students object to this state of affairs, but there is a strong drive to step aside from the conventional patterns and prohibitions and to work out, self-consciously, a new way of living with a group of people, accepting the inevitable wrangles, all-night soul searchings, and individual and collective self-doubts as a fair price for the intensity, intimacy, and self-discovery of a communal life.

Colleges could not sponsor communes if they wanted to. As soon as a commune becomes sponsored, it ceases to be a commune, I suppose. In any case, I have long been attracted by the by-product theory: namely, that important goods—for example, friendships and loves—often come on unannounced while one is concentrating on something else. If you set out deliberately in search of friendship or intimacy or an honest man, you may carry that lantern down a lot of lonely alleys. Perhaps this is an old man's skepticism: the testimonials from the young are hard to dispute. Though colleges have not gone communal, they have made dramatic accommodations to this second impulse. Who could have predicted, in 1960, the co-ed dormitories and open visting that now seems natural enough? Most colleges would consider it an act of grace if their dormitories should burn some night when everyone was on vacation. They could collect the insurance and build differently or perhaps provide concrete blocks, 2 x 4's, and plywood and let students invent their own shelters, learning some architecture along with psychology and sociology.

The third impulse driving away from the colleges has been discussed by Stafford North, and I will mention it only briefly. It is the arrival of an educational technology that emphasizes the clear definition of operational goals for the learning we hope to induce in students; the deliberate construction of more than one path to those goals; and the measurement of students' achievement before, during, and after the learning process. Any learning that can be analyzed into its component atoms can probably be taught without a classroom or a live teacher. Properly directed by books, television, computer-assisted instruction, and so on, a student can learn at his own pace, achieving the desired behavior as successfully as a student taking a course with others on a campus—or more successfully. Boyer and Keller, both at the State University of New York, make an impressive and balanced case for external degrees—learning carried out at home or elsewhere outside the classroom.[1] They lay out the great range and number of institutions that are now offering or crediting off-campus instruction at prices far below what one would pay to attend any one of our colleges.

Britain's new Open University, for example, hopes "to allow vast numbers of housewives and other adults with jobs to earn academic degrees in three to six years at a total cost to the student of less than $1,000. Last January, coal miners and clerks, salesmen and school teachers began enrolling in the Open University. . . . Thousands are listening to radio lectures, going through correspondence course packets, watching television courses, and reading in local libraries in preparation for examinations they will take at one of the 250 local study centers, where they also meet with some of the 2500 tutors and counselors who are acting as study assistants and advisers." [2]

[1] E. Boyer and G. Keller, "The Big Move to Non-Campus Colleges," *Saturday Review*, July 17, 1971, pp. 46–49, 58.

[2] Boyer and Keller, p. 48.

This is a large-scale operation, presumably using some of the techniques of programed instruction. And the same sort of thing is appearing in this country. The New York State Education Department has a much looser off-campus program: it will award an Associate in Arts or Bachelor in Business Administration degree to anyone who passes a set of comprehensive examinations, however he got his information. Thus one can get a degree without "enrolling at a college, setting a foot on a campus, or paying a penny in tuition." [3] Though private colleges, with a couple of exceptions, have taken little notice of this third force pulling away from the campus, it obviously will be a powerful one. It has economy and clarity on its side. I myself am not convinced that all learning can be reduced to its parts in such a way that it will be tractable to educational technology, and I think the environment of a campus is potentially too valuable to be abandoned. But without question this third vector will continue to pull away from us unless we can somehow turn it around.

I wonder if we can pull the colleges back together in this next decade, order our houses so that students find a really inviting outlet for their energy here instead of yearning out over the wall to another place where life is more varied or more intense or more efficient. I think it is possible; I even think the way to do it is becoming clear. We will not do it by a defensive insistence that we have been right all along and if students won't learn they can go vegetate somewhere else. Nor will we do it by transforming ourselves into a Woodstock or a Cistercian monastery or whatever is currently in favor with the young. We do need to come to terms with each of the three impulses I have spoken of—they are not trivial or evanescent. Though our visit to Decoy school reminds me that the quality of an environment does not necessarily lie in its structure, I would like to suggest three structural devices that may help us draw

[3] Boyer and Keller, p. 48.

back to the campus some of the energy that is directed elsewhere. They will not guarantee that all professors will fall into Sanford's admirable third type, but they may make it more difficult for our offerings to be dull, repetitive, or detached from the energy of ordinary lives or from the arguments and movements that animate the intellectual world.

The first two devices are relatively simple, already practiced by many colleges. First, we ought to make it easy and natural for students to drop out and drop in again. In fact, we need another name and another process so that they do not drop out at all; they take a leave of absence without severing their connections with the college. (I understand a number of colleges now make it possible for a student to drop out before he has even arrived by an admirable deferred admission plan.) The years from seventeen to twenty-three or twenty-four are unique. That is typically the only time in a person's life when he is no longer dependent (or not very dependent) on his family and does not yet have a family dependent on him. The students are right. They ought to use some of those years to try out unfamiliar settings and styles of life, and not all of this trying out can be done on campus. There is no need to sell those years to the future by following an unwavering course toward a career, as though the future would somehow disappear if one did not run to catch it. Second, a college ought to provide as great variety of places as it can. If the college is providing housing, let some of it be in dormitories and some in private houses; let some of the dormitories be co-ed and some segregated by sex; let some of the dormitories collect students in suites around a common living room while others offer the greater anonymity of single and double rooms down a corridor; let the students in some dorms or houses do their own cooking and housekeeping, even maintenance if they like. And let all of them make their places their own by painting murals on the stair wells.

Other places may be fully as important as living quarters

in defining the environment of a given student. My wife and I interviewed some Berea students in an attempt to discover what sort of environment the college is for them. (Incidentally, we recommend this informal interviewing to faculty and administrators. It is possible to teach for months or years and still have only a vague idea of the students' backgrounds and the ways in which the college affects them. Students talk freely; in an hour's interview one can often get a vivid sense of the shape and texture of their lives.) We asked each one what had happened to him since he had come to the college and what places he associated with these events, this change or growth. We were surprised how readily students do associate their significant experience with particular places and how sharply this geography differs from person to person. For one Berea girl, the important places were the pottery where she worked, the Firehouse (a coffeehouse in a building that used to be a fire station), and a room in the basement of her dormitory where she and four friends practiced karate every evening after supper. This may seem a strange collection of spaces, but each one connects convincingly with her past and with the changes she has undergone at Berea. Though she and another student lived in the same dormitory and attended classes in the same buildings, their "significant spaces" did not overlap at all. A college should be aware, as it improves its plant, that it may simply remove the places that are most important to some students. By modernizing and tidying up, it may homogenize the environment until it is difficult for a student to possess, psychologically, any space.

The third suggestion amounts to an unconventional plan for a curriculum, closely related, as you will see, to Evergreen State College's curriculum and Antioch's project-oriented studies, as Keeton has described them. (I am indebted to my colleague Laurence Barrett for the special combination of elements I am espousing.) Ordinarily in our courses we do two quite different things without distinguishing them very clearly.

We assign students various tasks, readings, or experiences intended to teach them certain things that we already know; and we also set them to explore or investigate things that neither they nor we understand very well in advance. Sometimes we join the students on problems of this second kind, working together to make some sense of whatever phenomenon it is we are interested in. My suggestion (or Professor Barrett's) is that we separate these two kinds of learning so that we can do each of them more effectively. That sounds simple enough, but if we did it in a thoroughgoing way it would mean a drastic change in the relationship between faculty member and student and in the whole character of our colleges.

Let me amplify this notion, briefly. For learning of the first type, where we know in advance the information and skills we hope students will acquire, why should we not bring to bear everything North and his colleagues have told us about educational technology? Why shouldn't we make clear the behavioral changes we hope to produce and devise the clearest and most efficient steps we can think of to help a student acquire the knowledge and skills we are aiming at? But let us do it in small pieces. Instead of expecting a student to pursue a chunk of programed learning for a whole term, let us divide it into modules that could be done in a couple of days of concentrated effort—and done when they are needed. One of these modules might be composed, perhaps, of directions and a certain amount of lecture on tape, plus readings, exercises, problems, experiments, mixed with frequent checks on what has been learned and opportunities to talk with someone about points that remain obscure. The effort of preparing these modules will be great, no doubt, though once they are well done they can be shared. And I admit it is not the kind of work I myself most enjoy. But I would be willing to do a module entitled "How to Read the Poems of John Donne" if someone else would help students get their bearings in seventeenth century English puritanism or pre-Copernican cosmology or the vortices of

Descartes' physics. I would make a module to help one become an effective interviewer if someone else would teach the student how to run the most common tests of statistical significance. These modules ideally will connect with the other half of the curriculum, the joint investigations. If students and I are trying to find out something about significant spaces on a campus it will help if we have the interview module and the statistical significance module at hand so that we do not have to take time out for that sort of routine instruction. Or if students and I are undertaking to compare Hieronymous Bosch and Franz Kafka, two religious wildmen, each with a surrealistic eye, we would hope there might be a module placing Bosch's work in the perspective of medieval artistic conventions, to speed us through that more straightforward preliminary learning.

My own enthusiasm is for this second half of the separated curriculum. If we can teach students briskly and clearly some of the things we already know, we should be able to give much more time than we now do to joint investigations, students and faculty working together on problems that genuinely interest and puzzle them both. We have been saying something like this off and on for a long time. Now we are beginning to produce convincing examples. Keeton has described eloquently three Antioch projects. All over the country faculty members and students are joining forces for investigations less dramatic than these, perhaps, but nonetheless marking a departure from the ordinary roles and procedures of a college course, calling up a new relationship between faculty and students, releasing a new reservoir of energy, and uncovering a new delight in learning. Everyone, it seems to me, is going on a 4-1-4 calendar or some variation of it, and the attraction is the *one,* the term when people can get together on a problem that is not in the catalog. Some are even going for 1-3-1-3-1 to get three times as many short terms.

I myself have taken pleasure in projects conventional in their timing and organization but still akin, I believe, to the winter-term projects that some of you have organized. For example, this last spring a colleague, Herbert Bogart, and I offered a contemporary poetry course in which we read the work of four poets, all of them now in mid-career. Every two weeks, after we had been reading and thinking about a poet's work, we brought him to campus for a poetry reading and informal talk with all of us. Though the course was large—over 100 students, many of them freshmen—and conventional in its structure, we did have a sense that we were discovering these poems together, puzzling our way through difficult passages, finding connections, sharing our fresh admiration for one poem or another. No one, at this moment, can safely claim to be expert in the work of John Logan, Galway Kinnell, Diane Wakoski, or Paul Backburn; if any of us were tempted to make pronouncements, we could be sure that the poet himself would show up in a week or two and deny everything.

Another example. A year and a half ago, a couple of colleagues and I (all of us English teachers) proposed what came to be called a space seminar. The subject was the arrangement of space and its relation to social patterns on college and university campuses. Students joined us. We discovered the literature on the subject, called for help from three architects, two anthropologists, and a psychologist, visited campuses, did analyses that ranged from pretty free speculation to some carefully conceived and surprisingly definitive studies. (Incidentally, we met in a different place each time.) Judging by student evaluations, morale in that seminar was higher than in any course I have been associated with. We worked extremely hard, but there was no feeling that the faculty were laying work on the students—the distinction between faculty and students was not pronounced, or at least the roles were not the conventional ones. The whole enterprise carried an air of exhilaration; we met a couple of times after the course was over, especially to hear students' observations about the use of space in Germany, Spain, and Sierra Leone, where they had been studying. We found, among other things, that we had grown fond of each other. There was nothing unique about the plan or circumstances of the seminar though the choice of subject did turn out to be a happy one. I am convinced the energy came from the sense of common investigation and discovery. I dare say similar investigations are appearing with similar excitement in almost every college in the country.

I am guessing that joint investigations, calling on carefully prepared modules for specific skills and blocks of information, will be the educational idea that takes hold in the 1970s as the idea of off-campus study took hold in the 1960s. I hope it may restore to the campuses some of the zeal that the sixties directed elsewhere. Among its other virtues, a joint investigation may, as a by-product, create close groups of students and faculty. Certainly, too, it will accord a new respect to our students, and this respect may work as powerfully on them as it has done on Lionel and Frankie Duff's students in Decoy, Kentucky.

Chapter 8

Marketing and Higher Education: Perspectives for Planning

Harold Mendelsohn

Today's higher education planners require a good deal of hard information that is not easily available. Counsel and guidance, also necessary, is all too easily available I am afraid. Yet, if we are to solve the problems that beset us in some rational way and if we are to plan ahead for survival the need to know is truly critical.

My particular task is to examine the possible analogs

that marketing and market research may present to the problems besetting independent liberal arts colleges today and then project some observations for the future of these institutions from those particular perspectives. In oversimplified terms the economic marketplace fundamentally is comprised of a four-variable mix: the producers of goods and services; the quality of the goods and services that are produced; the distributors of goods and services; and the ultimate consumers. The four variables are so delicately interrelated that changes in any one immediately affect the remaining elements in the mix in very significant ways.

In order to maintain the four variables in functional balance, particularly within a sharply competitive marketplace, business enterprises devote substantial amounts of time, talent, energy, and money to planning, research and development, product testing, and consumer research as a routine adjunct to their everyday activity. Not to plan ahead, not to develop and test new products of services, and simply to take the opinion pulses of their customers occasionally, or not to bother studying them at all, is to invite economic disaster. Interesting to note are the roles that our colleges and universities have played in abetting industry in maintaining a viable economic marketplace for its goods and services. Yet, how much of the activity engaged in by our colleges and universities is oriented routinely to planning, research and development, evaluation of curriculum, and researching student characteristics, needs, expectations, attitudes, and satisfactions and dissatisfactions as they apply directly to the activity of acquiring a college education? Very little, indeed. And what little effort of this sort does occur is usually haphazard, amateurish, variable, ad hoc, and, even more disturbing, post hoc, in nature. Curiously, while colleges and universities have devoted considerable energy to the maintenance of a workable economic marketplace, they have been seriously neglecting their own enterprise—the educational marketplace. And now that higher education is in trouble we desperately run about seeking the information that we should have been gathering systematically and routinely over the past one hundred years in much the same manner that the ancients beseeched the Delphic Oracle. And, I might add—with about the same results.

In the marketplace of higher education we encounter a similar four-variable mix: the producers of educational materials, curricula, and programs; the materials, programs, and curricula that are offered; the methods and techniques of disseminating these materials; and the consumer-student. Although each of these variables deserves considerable serious attention, I shall focus upon one—the actual consumers of higher education, the students. In focusing upon the potential and actual markets for higher education we inevitably touch upon other factors constituting the higher education marketplace. And perhaps when we do, we shall begin to see how the one directly affects the others in consequential ways.

What is fashionably referred to currently as the "crisis in higher education" is a direct consequence of a long-term cherished American dream—the achievement of universal education. Great strides toward fulfilling this dream have been made, although, as is the case with all dream-fulfillment exercises, the results have not always been entirely functional. Surely none of us is unfamiliar with the statistics that chronicle the escalating student population. This growth has reached the point where, in 1970, there were 14.5 million students enrolled in high school—93.7 per cent of those eligible (fourteen- to seventeen-year-olds). At the same time, the illiteracy rate has dropped below 2.4 per cent among those over fourteen. In higher education the shock-wave increases in student enrollment can be measured by decades rather than by generations. From 1960 to 1970 college enrollment figures leaped from 3,600,000 to 7,600,000. It is possible that college enrollment in the next decade will approach fifteen million.

The push towards higher education reflects itself in more

than the near-geometric increases in enrollment, staff, and facilities. Whereas in 1960, 41 per cent of all degree-seeking students attended private institutions of higher education, this proportion fell to 27 per cent in 1970. Projections for 1980 indicate that it will have dropped to about 19 per cent by then. At the same time the annual costs of educating a student enrolled in a private institution will have more than doubled (from $1,506 in 1960 to a projected $3,208 in 1980). The projected increases for student education in public institutions are not quite as alarming (from $1,456 in 1960 to a projected $2,256 in 1980).

From these gross market figures we can readily define at least one major dilemma that faces the private institutions of higher learning. As the market for higher education has changed its essential character from "class" to "mass," the share of that market, as far as privately controlled institutions are concerned, has been diminishing and will continue to do so in the face of increasing costs to the consumer. Given such circumstances the options open to privately controlled colleges and universities are extremely limited. In fact, only two alternatives are feasible: private institutions can attempt either to reverse the trend or to halt it. Either option calls for considerable alternation in each of the four variables comprising the current higher educational market mix, and the privately controlled college or university may find itself reconstituting its structural and functional attributes almost entirely.

Because diminishing shares of the market are warnings of impending catastrophe, any business firm confronted with such a development first will compare its products or services to those of its competitors and carefully examine its customers' habits, attitudes, experiences with its products or services, as well as their reasons for switching. This will be accompanied by a thorough examination of management, financing, production modes, distribution systems, pricing policies, and communications. More often than not, it becomes clear that a gap between the product or service offered and consumer needs and expectations has opened and widened. In recent years these discrepancies are reflected chiefly in greater differentiations in individual and subpopulation tastes than in any other factor. This means that as one-time heterogeneous mass markets begin to segmentalize themselves on the basis of sex, age, socio-economic status, values, tastes, life-styles, educational achievement levels, occupational status, and so on into identifiable subgroupings with specific shared attributes, producers of goods and services begin to tailor their products and services accordingly. Rather than viewing potential consumers as one undifferentiated mass which is to be presented with but one purchasing option, contemporary producers present potential consumers with a smorgasbord of commodities and services from which they may select those best suited to their peculiar dispositions and circumstances.

The paradox looming before us when we turn to the higher education marketplace is the emergence of a mass market from what used to be a rather differentiated and highly selected one. While the economic marketplace has gradually been segmentalizing its consumers, the potential higher education market appears many primarily as an undifferentiated mass of what is simplistically labeled "eligible high school graduates." Accordingly, the educational fare is frequently undifferentiated and the typical college student has very little leeway in exercising his individual preferences. In reality, of course, today's student market is essentially heterogeneous and differentiated and our frantic efforts to accommodate the mass market while offering lip-service to individual needs has almost guaranteed the perpetuation of even greater homogenization of higher educational fare. Perhaps the most ostensible example is the standardized and inflexible teaching inputs that now comprise much of our so-called instructional media. I am not saying that we should ignore the dissemination potential of instructional media in reaching a mass student market. This may be a temporary means of economically accommodating the tens of thousands of students now pouring into the universities. What I do find objectionable is the tendency in some sectors of higher education to equate the ability of *some* instructional media to facilitate *some* very circumscribed aspects of the learning process with the media's supposed power to afford *all* students an "individualized" learning experience. Certainly, if college students today are indeed expressing a desire for a personalized individual learning experience, propping them up before a screen that flashes the exact same prefabricated, canned, educational gumbo to one and all cannot be expected to fulfill such a preference.

The marketing game has been for institutions to compete fiercely for students who are best qualified both intellectually—as measured by standardized test—and financially. Doermann has investigated the futility of this competition and demonstrates that this particular demographic pool is so shallow as to be a goldfish pond, not the inland sea one might believe.[1] Doermann's figures show for example that no more than 2.7 per cent of all high school graduates from households with gross annual incomes of $16,200 (who, presumably, can contribute a yearly minimum of $3,000 toward an offspring's college education) scored 550 or better on their verbal S.A.T.'s. On the lower rungs of the gross family income ladder Doermann's data are even more disheartening: high verbal S.A.T. performers (550 or better) comprise no more than two-fifths of 1 per cent of the high school graduates from households which gross less than $7,500 annually and which presumably could contribute less than $730 each year to an offspring's college education. Put another way, among the 1,450,000 high school graduates who took verbal S.A.T.'s in 1969–1970, there were 80,000 who scored 550 or better and could best afford to pay for a college education. There were 22,000 students who scored best but

[1] H. Doermann, "The Student Market for Private Colleges," *Liberal Education,* May 1970, 56:*2,* 292–304.

could least afford to finance their higher education. Altogether, regardless of ability to pay, no more than 166,000 high school graduates scored 550 or better on the verbal S.A.T.'s in 1969–1970. This represents 11.5 per cent of all students graduating from high school that year.

Doermann's figures suggest that the current and projected pressures for increased college enrollment are not coming from the best qualified students (as measured by standard tests) nor from those who can simultaneously meet the increased costs of higher education in private or in many of public institutions: "The nation's largest unsolved educational and social problem in higher education lies in the large group of students of average and below-average measured aptitude who also receive substantial financial aid if they are to attend any college."[2] For many colleges and universities the capacity to resolve this fundamental dilemma very well may spell the difference between survival and extinction.

Implicit in Doermann's investigation is the necessity for considerable restructuring: from developing new criteria for academic aptitude to lowering the admission sights of institutions that persist in aiming only at the highest scorers; from reexamining costs, fees, curricula, and personnel to showing more concern for the differentiable needs and aspirations of the majority of student candidates who are but modestly endowed, both intellectually and financially. Like it or not higher education is being forced to acknowledge differences in its own structures, functions, and "products" in response to the growing segmentalization of its students. The time is not too distant when students will choose an institution for its uniqueness rather than for its efforts to simulate as closely as possible some medieval prototype. Two conditions must exist for students to exercise their choices on the basis of the unique qualities of an institution: if institutions begin to develop realistic objec-

[2] Doermann, p. 296.

tives congruent with their peculiarly unique capabilities and if the means of paying for both private and public higher education is changed. It is clear that the latter condition calls for considerable redeployment of public revenues in both the private and public sectors, perhaps not so much to the institutions themselves, as has been the case, but directly to potential and matriculated students who will have an opportunity to exercise their own preferences regarding the institutions they wish to attend.

Suppose the impossible dream regarding ample financing somehow becomes real. Our dilemma is still far from over. Institutions will have to acknowledge the necessity of carving out that unique segment of the higher education market which will keep them in business, so to speak, and to do this they must know the student market as never before. A recent flood of materials allegedly dissecting the contemporary college student has been emanating from such observers as Reich, Keniston, Toffler, Drucker, and Roszack, to name a few. Seminal and provocative as these observations may be, they all suffer from the same shortcoming—they are both subjective and speculative. Moreover they reflect short-term, singular impressions rather than long-term trend observations, and we rarely encounter in these Delphic prognostications hard facts gathered over a statistically respectable length of time; it is precisely such trend information that is needed. For example, we need to know the explicit manpower needs of our society over the next generation, what occupations will phase out, which new ones will take their place, what new skills will be needed, and which old skills will become obsolete. We need precise demographic, sociological, political, cultural, and economic data to map out the future contours of American society. We need to flesh out typologies of future students not only according to ideological and political criteria but also as reflections of values, attitudes, aspirations, life styles, and motivations as they relate explicitly to the pursuit of a college education. For example, what proportions of the student market are vocation- and job-oriented; what proportions seek satisfaction and fulfillment in the pursuit of abstract intellectualism, in the arts, in political and social activism, in industry, and in the helping and healing vocations? We need to know which subgroups are tradition-oriented as well as those which are innovative in their value dispositions; which must remain near home and which look forward to leaving, which find the pursuit of education in our giant urban institutions an exciting prospect, and which look forward to the rewards of smaller institutions in less populated areas. We need to know for which types of students the two-year, four-year and post-graduate academic programs will be best.

In general, the variables to be examined in determining student preferences are two-fold, representing the internal-psychological as well as the external-environmental. The model for study is that used by many social researchers and marketing experts: behavior is a function of the interactions between internal and external stimuli and, simultaneously, between rational and irrational processes. It can be assumed that these interactions are primary determinants of whether persons of certain definable and measurable characteristics, attributes, and dispositions will seek a college education, choose a particular institution and a given program or curriculum, and actually achieve a higher education within given periods of time. What seems to be called for, in addition to a thorough knowledge of the basic characteristics of the market, is a deeper understanding of the decision processes which move students into and through the various means of achieving a college education. Thus far we know very little about these processes and their dynamics. If it is true that colleges and universities—particularly those in the private sector—will be differentiating their offerings so they will be more congruent with student preferences, it will be imperative to discern the existing preferences. This is extremely important in terms of both planning for changes and in terms of communicating with prospective students as well as with those already on campus. In pragmatic marketing terms the liberal arts college of the future will have to develop a unique identity which is congruent with unique constellations of student attributes that are more reflective of a particular student-consumer subgroup than they are of the total student-consumer universe. Additionally, unless institutions can communicate their unique approaches to a given student's educational needs and expectations, they will fail to attract the very students they plan to serve.

For purposes of discussion let us concentrate briefly on those qualified persons who have decided "to go to college." I use the term "qualified" operationally in the realization that this concept itself needs considerable reexamination. To help us recognize how a given student may go about choosing a particular college or university we find the consumer decision model developed by Nicosia of the University of California at Berkeley a promising analog.[2]

Nicosia divides the decision process into four "fields." Field One represents the processes by which (in this instance) a particular college or university comes to the attention of a potential student and affects certain of his predispositions. Here the dynamics of communications predominate: the institution disseminates messages about itself and its attributes, seeking out those with the attributes which will allow them to pick up the messages, understand them, and begin to incorporate them. Actual incorporation occurs in Field Two, which Nicosia terms the "pre-action field." Here the messages funnel through a wide variety of internal-psychological and external-environmental filters until the messages reach those for whom they were intended and the recipients perceives the messages in the manner intended. If this process encounters no obstacles the messages become relevant and act as a direct input in the formation of

[2] F. Nicosia, *Consumer Decision Processes* (Englewood Cliffs, New Jersey: Prentice-Hall, 1966).

positive attitudes toward the sender-institution. If, however, there is "noise" in the system the messages may be either ignored and lost or stored for future use. The formation of a relevant attitude assumes the aspect of a positive motivation towards the institution in question. At this point the prospective student begins "searching" into his own psyche as well as into the environment for rationales that will support and re-enforce his ultimate decision. During the search process the student also conducts a means-ends evaluation in terms of his own needs and the institution's ability to meet them.

Field Three is concerned with the overt act of choice as a result of a charged-up motivation. Nicosia describes what occurs in Field Three in economic marketing terms:

> *The input into Field Three is the motivation emerging as the output of Field Two. This motivation is a cognitive structure whose scope is very differentiated and specific, and whose dynamics drives the subject strongly toward an overt act of choice; it is a structure that identifies at least one brand as the more visible or preferable means toward the solution of the consumer's problem. Therefore, the consumer will strongly tend to initiate activities that may lead to the purchase of the preferred brand.*[3]

Before acting, however, the subject will seek more information from both his own psychological and experiential repertoires and from external sources. Only when external realities (for example, the existence of a specific curriculum or program in a given institution) are congruent with the internal search findings will the decision be made. Otherwise, discrepancies in the two systems will lead to a break-off of the actual behavioral decision. Field Four mainly is concerned with the

[3] Nicosia.

feedback the institution receives from those students who have decided to attend, what it does with that information, and likewise with the student's experience with the institution. These double outcomes act as new inputs into the decisions of future students.

As our institutions in higher education learn more about their own students and the manner in which they make their academically-related decisions, they will become more sensitive to themselves as institutions. This does not mean that college and university policy should address itself solely and precipitously to student demands. Rather, more intensive study of the student-consumer may actually uncover the underlying bases for many of the more overt expressions of student dissatisfaction that institutions now encounter. Such knowledge can serve as a realistic guide to adjustments in programs and curricula, enabling institutions to delineate their targets in precise terms and to fashion pertinent programs, curricula, and communications accordingly.

Unless each of our institutions of higher learning, in concert with its counterparts around the country, dedicates itself to an on-going study, review, and evaluation of the higher education market—with a strong emphasis on the student-consumer—many of our fine colleges and universities will fail. As we seek more reliable information about each variable in the educational market; as we shed traditional assumptions; as we begin to recognize that each institution must capitalize on its unique resources; as more and more students are given opportunities to exercise their motivations and preferences—in short, as higher education begins to adopt rational techniques for planning a healthy future—we shall begin to progress toward the resolution of the pressing problems challenging higher education today. As we do so, we shall help to resolve the problems facing society tomorrow.

Chapter 9

Rescuing the Small College: A Bold Approach

Earl J. McGrath

Throughout their more than three-hundred year history liberal arts colleges have had recurrent ups and downs. Now, however, with notable exceptions, these venerable institutions are beset by financial exigencies of unprecedented proportions. Moreover, the critical situation in which the colleges now find themselves has been caused in considerable part by irreversible forces. Barring unforeseeable changes in established social, economic, and political doctrines, the ameliorative steps that might ordinarily be considered feasible cannot now be as effective. Tuition and other fees cannot be reduced to widen the potential market; individual salaries and fringe benefits cannot be materially lowered to contract expenditures; maintenance costs and debt charges cannot be substantially cut back to offset current deficits. In fact, if the practices of the past decade continue, all the foregoing and other items of expense will become even more burdensome. No useful purpose can be served by still another dramatic recital of the dismal situation, however, and the purpose of the present review is not to sound the tocsin again, but rather to offset some of the pervasive gloom and inertia. It is hoped that by providing practical, though not always palatable, courses of action, some of the conditions which are sapping the vitality of these institutions may be alleviated.

The first step toward a reversal of present trends toward insolvency ought be a realistic recognition that the usual sources of assistance will no longer suffice. Except during periods of severe economic stringency, institutions faced with the necessity of meeting deficits have typically looked outward for additional revenue. Tuition fees have been steadily raised; previous benefactors have been urged to augment their largesse; new donors have been sedulously pursued; emotional appeals have been made to alumni to save their alma mater, and in recent years, dramatic appeals to corporations have become the custom. None of these former fountainheads of sustenance can singly or combined meet the predictable financial needs of the colleges. Indeed, unless reforms are instituted to improve the economics of institutional operation, some of the support from these traditional sources will also melt away.

Tuition fees, for example, have already reached a point of diminishing return. Even families with ten to fifteen thousand dollar incomes cannot meet the rising tuition charges. Moreover, today's students who, unlike their predecessors, have access to budget information are beginning to realize that in a college which spends several hundred thousand dollars of its own funds for scholarship assistance, a significant portion of their own tuition payments pays for the education of their classmates. Even socially-minded students now wonder whether this is an equitable aid plan. The few colleges which for years have had a waiting line for admission may be able to continue to raise their fees with impunity (though this may be questionable social policy); as Doermann has so convincingly shown, however, in others the total income from fees may fall rather than rise with further tuition increases.[1]

Individual philanthropists may be expected to continue their gifts, and all enterprising colleges will energetically pursue these potential benefactions. There are thousands of millionaires, as well as many others whose fortunes are small but whose incomes are large, who in spite of available tax deductions make no significant donations to any private institution, either during life or at death. Persistent search for these "sleepers" will be rewarding to convincing petitioners for college support. But few institutions can expect such windfalls. Moreover, private donors are becoming more discriminating in their philanthropies; very few can be expected to give their money to offset deficit spending.

Corporations and their officers, many of whom serve on college boards of trustees, are showing increasing concern about the financial management of the colleges which are their prospective beneficiaries. They cannot look with favor on the requests of institutions which consistently budget deficits and businessmen will be naturally skeptical about the future of a college which uses its endowment or other capital funds to disguise what would be treated in business as an operating loss. One large corporation, which for years has made hundreds of

[1] H. Doermann, "The Student Market for Private Colleges," in *Cross-Currents in College Admissions* (New York: Teachers College Press, 1970).

gifts to colleges and universities on an across-the-board basis, has adopted the more discerning policy of trying to evaluate the way in which its funds are likely to be spent. This policy is not designed to abridge the right of an institution to determine its own purposes and programs but rather to question whether its resources are being economically employed to reach professed goals. In the years ahead, this practice may be expected to become standard among corporations.

Foundations have uniformly followed the policy of supporting institutions which design and execute imaginative educational innovations. Only under extraordinary circumstances have these agencies bailed out those incapable of making financial ends meet. Colleges in serious financial trouble, therefore, can expect little or no help from foundations. Moreover, it has not been the policy of most foundations to commit themselves indenfinitely to any project, no matter how meritorious. The primary reason is that if the new enterprise has merit it should, within a period of several years, be able to justify its continuous support from institutional resources. Few if any colleges can therefore expect to solve their long-range financial problems by attracting foundation support.

For many years alumni have steadily increased their giving to the point that in some notable institutions the annual contributions from graduates equal the income on an endowment of ten million dollars or more. In most colleges, however, such income constitutes only a small fraction of the annual budget and cannot be expected to significantly offset prospective deficits. Moreover, to match federal building grants, some colleges have importuned their alumni so steadily for special capital gifts that the funds needed to sustain a high quality instructional program have shrunk. Like private donors, corporations, and foundations, alumni will have little interest in contributing their income to wipe out back debts.

This review of prospective donors leads to the ineluctable conclusion that to remain solvent few private colleges can expect indefinitely to obtain sufficient funds from traditional sources. Most college presidents have already accepted the fact that traditional sources will not continue to provide sufficient funds, and trustees are rapidly coming to the same troubling conclusion. It is because of this awareness, and the recognition that they have already taken the first steps down the road to complete financial breakdown, that some boards of trustees have already taken two unprecedented, and for some, unpleasant actions. Many trustees, especially those in high corporate offices, have resisted the increasingly common practice among the colleges of turning to the government to solve their financial problems. Because they are convinced that the aggregate income from the usual sources will not be sufficient to preserve the institution for which they are legally and morally responsible, many trustees now join in urging legislators to provide urgently needed help. They do so, however, with the recognition that government grants can at best be modest in terms of current needs.

Trustees know too that if government should accept a large measure of responsibility for the continuing support of the private colleges, these institutions eventually would become essentially public educational agencies, subject to all the policies and controls now imposed on their state counterparts. They rightly fear that some priceless features of our system would be lost. (Anyone who has any doubts on this subject should read *University Independence,* a recent work by a group of distinguished British scholars who review the intrusions of the British government, through the Universities Grants Committee, into such ancient academic institutions as Oxford and Cambridge.) [2]

Trustees with large corporate responsibilities are uneasy about soliciting substantial government support because they believe such grants may only serve to becloud one of the chief

[2] J. H. MacCallum Scott (Ed.), *University Independence* (London: Rex Collings, 1971).

causes of the present economic crisis—the uneconomical use of existing resources. In this view they are joined by government officers in both the executive and legislative branches. Several liberal governors, dedicated to the extension of higher education and the enhancement of its quality, have nevertheless expressed the view that unless these institutions are operated more efficiently, the taxpayers will simply not provide the funds required to meet their budgets. (Two of these executives were assuming that their states would have to provide substantial assistance in one form or another to privately supported institutions.) To one listener, at least, these executives were predicting that the states would apply the same standards of efficient management to both private and public colleges and universities. Those who believe that government aid will solve the financial problems of private institutions by enabling them to continue their business on the customarily casual basis are destined to be sorely disappointed. The inescapable conclusion is that most colleges must look inward toward more economical use of the resources they have (although, to be sure, they must continue to seek aid from all conceivable patrons).

The facts indicate clearly, however, that even persons committed to helping these institutions will more and more be inclined to support colleges which are able to present detailed facts showing that they are not seeking additional funds to sustain practices inefficient and wasteful. No longer will contributors be convinced of institutional need by such general statements as "We need a new science building or a new library." Or such Micawber-like forecasts as "We expect larger enrollments and therefore need additional dormitories or a larger auditorium." Or "We need a larger faculty because individualized instruction requiring small classes and personal contacts results in greater intellectual growth and personal development." These vague, generalized statements will have to be replaced by facts and plans related to sound management policies and procedures, such statements as "The curriculum has been pared down to a minimum consistent with the proper goals of an undergraduate college" and "The student-faculty ratio has been raised to 20 to 1" and "The use of instructional space has been raised to the point of making additional facilities unnecessary."

Whether an institution's resources are used effectively can only be discovered by determining whether they are spent for purposes which are clearly expressed and understood by all members of the academic community. All those using its money —in the administrative offices, in the classroom, library, or laboratory, on the athletic field—must not only comprehend these goals, they must be committed to the task of reaching them. The purposes of an institution generally have not been translated into the daily activities of the campus. Little of the elegant catalog rhetoric on objectives leads to modifications in the substance of courses, the methods of teaching, or in campus life generally. No hope can be held out for assessing the efficiency with which funds are spent until there is some consensus on the kinds of goals the college is trying to reach. The first step toward the necessary clarification of purposes is the reestablishment of the idea that the function of the liberal arts college is a distinctive one in the system of higher education.

Declaring Independence and Intent

To the end of reestablishing their own identity, the colleges ought to disavow their vassalage and subservience to any and all other members of the academic establishment. They ought to affirm their intellectual and moral independence of the graduate schools, the professional colleges, and the professional accrediting associations, all of which now directly or indirectly impose on the liberal arts college policies and practices inimical to their well being. Such a declaration would at once serve notice on the other units in the academic establisment and inform the public at large that the college has an integrity of its own. If such a statement were prepared and endorsed by all members of the college community, it would transfer professional loyalties from extramural organizations back to the college community as an entity and publicity commit its adherents to the proposition that the college had irrevocably resolved to stand or fall on the validity of its own mission. Far better that a college should fail on its own terms than survive in ignominious pretension.

A position of such independence will require stern decisions involving the entire membership of the college community—the trustees, administration, faculty, students, and extramural supporters as well. The demanding task of reestablishing a defensible set of purposes for liberal arts colleges ought not be left solely or even principally to any one of these constituent groups. The dominant goals as well as the character and quality of American life are so deeply involved in these decisions on purposes that no one social group ought to be given the responsibility of making such fateful decisions. Even if it were morally defensible to vest such enormous power in a single body, none of these groups, as presently constituted, is alone qualified to discharge the attendant responsibilities. If, however, a body representing all the groups properly concerned with the welfare of a college were to be legally constituted, it should be able to reach sound agreements on all major institutional purposes consistent with the comprehensive objectives of American society. It might be hoped, also, that agreement could be reached on the specific services to which the college ought to commit itself.

Any analysis of the chaotic condition of contemporary life suggests that the dominant mission of the college must be the education of youth to live effective personal lives while discharging the responsibilities of enlightened citizenship in a democracy. Although there are ubiquitous endorsements of this high goal, the dominant motivations and activities of the profession as a whole in recent years have not been moving toward its achievement. No basic educational reforms can be expected in smaller liberal arts colleges while the mores of academic society discourage this kind of commitment. The practice of rewarding those who achieve distinction in other spheres of professional activity—research, publications, prominence in scholarly organizations or outside consultative activities—has encouraged an alienation from teaching. Reorientation of purpose and concomitant reordering of the system of rewards would facilitate a long needed reconstruction of the curriculum. Undergraduate institutions should be able to drop, for example, many advanced specialized courses which serve the interests of teachers more than students. The time of faculty members thus released could be used to improve the basic courses which should constitute the indispensible elements in a genuine liberal education.

Several careful studies have shown that with notable exceptions liberal arts colleges offer too many courses. Moreover, the relationship between the number of students enrolled and the number of different courses taught is not close. In the early 1960s the curricular offerings of a number of colleges were reviewed. This analysis revealed that in roughly comparable institutions of national reputation the number of credit hours of instruction offered varied from 1278 to 2131, a difference of 853 hours. Since a course typically carried three semester hours credit, these figures mean that one college offered 284 more courses (not sections) than another. More significantly, two colleges with quite comparable enrollments varied widely in the range of their offerings. One with 785 students thought that it could provide an adequate program with only 1278 hours of instruction, while another with only 59 more students believed it had to schedule 2039 credit hours, 761 hours, or, at three semester hours per course, 254 more courses than its sister institution. It is not surprising that the average class size in the college with the richer curricular menu was fifteen compared with twenty-four in the college with the leanest offering. The fiscal consequences of this extravagant proliferation of courses need no documentation.

Viewing these and other facts related to the needless expansion of the instructional offerings in colleges of arts and sciences, I expressed the following opinion concerning the long-range deleterious results of this practice:

> *Severe financial problems related to the curriculum already exist in the independent liberal arts colleges. Indeed, their status in the structure of higher education and in the whole of American society now rests in the balance. The outcome will be determined very largely by the willingness of faculty members to view the entire life of the college objectively, including their own special interests. To the degree that they put the general welfare above departmental and personal considerations the well-being of the liberal arts colleges will be maintained. If they do not do this, these institutions will languish as some have already begun to do. Moreover, if the crisis deepens without appropriate faculty action, the tradition of faculty control of the curriculum will necessarily be abrogated by those who have the legal and moral responsibility to preserve and advance the welfare of these colleges.*[3]

No one attempting to reexamine the purposes of American higher education in relation to the conditions in American society should approach the task without first acquainting himself with John L. Holland's pivotal studies in this area. These impeccable investigations of the relationship between the abilities possessed by high school graduates and their success in college and later life show the inadequacy of admissions criteria

[3] E. J. McGrath, *Memo to a College Faculty Member* (New York: Bureau of Publications, Teachers College, Columbia University, 1961), p. vi.

limited solely to such academic qualifications as high school grades and entrance examinations. Such scores leave unexposed a wide range of qualities of mind and personality which in fact are also related to later achievement. Measures of scholastic and nonacademic traits and abilities do not significantly intercorrelate. Hence, the application of limited academic criteria results in the rejection of many applicants who would predictably succeed not only in a narrow scholastic sense but also in other life activities of equal social value. Holland summarizes the significance of his research as follows:

> *The results imply a need for a broader, or different, definition of both the nature of human talent and the nature of higher education. There are many kinds of human accomplishment, and each kind is likely to benefit from some type of higher education, although not necessarily a highly academic type. In other words, our results imply a need for a wide variety of colleges, many, if not most of them, relatively unselective except on dimensions clearly relevant to their particular emphasis. Measures of academic and nonacademic accomplishment would then be used in selecting students for a single college.*[4]

Those colleges dedicated to enhancing their social value, if they give proper weight to the practical implications of these findings, will reexamine their selection policies. In any reevaluation of these processes, they will want to consider accepting freshmen who in the aggregate differ considerably from those admitted or rejected under the more restrictive and discriminating policies of recent years. Many institutions can solve their fiscal problems only by attracting more students; this, in turn,

[4] J. M. Richards, Jr., J. L. Holland, and S. W. Lutz, *Prediction of Student Accomplishment in College,* ACT Research Report, 1966, 13, 353–354.

may be possible only if they open their doors to students with a broader range of personal traits and abilities. They will unquestionably draw many students of real potential from among those now rejected by their academically status-conscious competitors.

The unit costs of instruction in the courses offered in the upper two years of most college programs considerably exceed the costs of those predominantly attended by freshmen and sophomores. These cost differentials result in part from the fact that senior members of the staff typically give the advanced courses attended by relatively few students, usually the departmental majors. In colleges of one thousand or fewer students, other forces of equal economic significance are at work. For a variety of reasons—changing intellectual interests, lack of money, disappointment in their college experiences, marriage, outright failure, among others—a considerable number of students fail to return at the end of the freshman and sophomore years. Consequently, in the absence of transfers into the junior and senior years, upper class enrollments drop and the inevitably smaller classes mean a commensurate rise in the cost of instruction. Although colleges vary considerably in the distribution of general requirements over the four-year undergraduate period, the courses which must be pursued by all degree candidates are taken in the first two years. This practice increases the size of classes at the lower levels, but tends to reduce class size in the junior and senior years with a further rise in the unit cost of instruction. The requirement that every student elect a sequence of advanced courses in his major field causes a further scattering of registrations. In an institution which provides twenty major options for a class of two hundred graduates, the resulting average of ten majors will mean that many classes will enroll ten or fewer students, and, of course, majors are never distributed evenly. The offering of a multitude of advanced courses in a single major field further reduces the size of classes.

One obvious device for assuring an increase in average class size in the upper two years is to increase the enrollments in the freshman class while making the program sufficiently attractive to hold until graduation a larger percentage of those admitted. Even with the most effective efforts to reduce drop-outs, however, significant attrition is unavoidable. If, therefore, the senior and junior classes are to approximate those in the lower two years, thereby reducing the average unit cost of instruction, means must be found to attract students who have already completed two years of college education elsewhere.

The community colleges are a largely unexploited source of such students. That the youngest of our institutions of higher education has become an important and permanent unit in the system is attested to by its rapid growth. Although the figures for the early years may not be exact when compared with those for recent decades, they do reveal the vigorous growth of this institution. In 1900 only eight institutions classified as junior colleges (the forerunner of the community college), with a total enrollment of approximately 100 students. By 1920 the number had risen to 207 and the attendance to twelve thousand. Twenty years later 467 such institutions enrolled 200,000 students. By 1960 the figures had become 678 and 660,000 respectively. The spectacular growth, however, occurred in two five-year periods from 1960 to 1970. By 1965 there were 837 community colleges with enrollments of 1,288,000, and five years later 1091 colleges could boast 2.5 million enrollees.

Most four-year colleges have not yet adequately exploited the potentially rich resource of community college graduates. Because of class feelings at the "upper" levels of academic society and the fear of losing status in the establishment, in fact, some colleges have deliberately refrained from trying to attract community college graduates. Since transfers from community colleges to top-ranking universities do as well as or better than their own students, this policy reveals a peculiar lack of enterprise.

The establishment of community colleges in the regions from which the four-year colleges have traditionally drawn their patronage, however, has caused the more recent arrivals to be viewed as unwanted competitors. The extent to which the public community college, with its easy geographical, academic, and financial accessibility, has actually drawn off the prospective patrons of four-year institutions has not been reliably determined. The community college cannot be wished away, at any rate, and the colleges that accept this fact of contemporary academic life and capitalize on it may, in fact, be able to turn an apparent liability into an actual asset. Transfers from community colleges may enable the four-year institutions to reduce the present debilitating instructional costs of small junior and senior classes. To gain this fiscal advantage, however, they will have to launch recruiting activities among the seniors in the community colleges with the same vigor and imagination now devoted to similar efforts among high school graduates. Even with maximum effort to attract students a severe barrier to this movement would remain: the cost of attending a private college is substantially higher than a state university.

A Minnesota study revealed that of two thousand students in the second year of the community colleges, 2.5 per cent were planning transfer to a private college. If, however, the costs had been equalized, 47 per cent said that they would transfer to such an institution. Colleges which now spend hundreds of thousands of dollars for scholarship aid to high school graduates might fruitfully use a portion of their severely limited financial resources to attract community college graduates. Most of the latter, in contrast to those who have had no college experience, could reasonably be expected to complete the requirements for a degree. The prudent expenditure of such funds to bring students of demonstrated ability, achievement, and motivation into the upper courses of the various disciplines is a policy which deserves much more consideration than it has commonly received.

The intensification of our space efforts after 1957 caused many institutions to increase their outlays for plant facilities in substantial proportions by erecting completely new, or by renovating and adding to old, structures. Since these facilities were often made possible through federal grants and loans carrying low interest rates and long-term repayment options many institutions which could have got on with existing structures were unable to resist the seduction. And since Congressional legislation provided aid largely for science buildings, which typically cost much more than other structures, the financial burden for many has turned out to be inordinately heavy. Many colleges which cannot, and indeed should not, make any pretension to substantial scientific research, find themselves with elaborate facilities, beautifully appointed, efficiently instrumented, but with relatively few students in their laboratories or classrooms. Not uncommonly the departments of chemistry, physics, and geology which occupy these monuments to a baseless academic affluence produce each year an aggregate of a dozen majors. (Since the biological sciences provide instruction for large numbers of students who intend to take advanced degrees in the health sciences their production record is more satisfactory.)

It would be prejudicial, however, to assess the prudence and economic feasibility of recent construction solely in terms of the scientific departments. With federal and state help colleges have erected thousands of dormitories, libraries, and student unions to be amortized over extended periods. These public loans usually have had to be complemented by funds from corporations, alumni, and other private benefactors. These enterprising activities, calculated to provide larger and better physical facilities, have imposed heavy debt service and maintenance charges which colleges met during the recent period of easy money with minimum financial strain.

The financial consequences of these burdens have not been fully realized. They become obvious in Table 1 which illustrates the situation in one highly-reputable Midwestern

TABLE 1

Science Majors in a Midwestern College 1961–62 to 1970–71

Department	1961–62	1964–65	1967–68	1970–71	Growth or Shrinkage %
Biology	7	14	14	15	114 (+)
Chemistry	7	5	3	6	14.3 (–)
Geology	3	3	5	4	33.3 (+)
Physics	15	8	8	3	80.0 (–)
Total	32	30	30	28	6.3 (–)
Full Time Enrollment	837	977	1347	1286	53.6 (+)
Full Time Faculty in College	55	65	83	87	58.2 (+)
FullTime Science Faculty	8.5	11.5	14.5	17	100.0 (+)

college in severe financial difficulty. In this institution enrollments increased from 837 to 1286, or 53.6 per cent, from 1961–1962 to 1970–1971. During the same period, however, science majors dropped from thirty-two to twenty-eight; if biology is excluded the drop becomes catastrophically significant, from twenty-three to thirteen. This contraction, however, is paralleled by a crushing expansion in the faculty in these departments. In 1961–1962 there were only 8.5 members in the four science departments, but by 1970–1971 this figure had exactly doubled. Comparing the two sets of figures it appears that while the faculty figure was rising in chemistry, geology, and physics from 5.5 to 12, or 118 per cent, the majors were dropping from 25 to 13, or 48 per cent. And the total institutional enrollment was rising by 53.6 per cent. The impact of these developments on the total institutional financial situation was intensified by the erection of a science building, at a cost of three million dollars, near the end of this period when enrollments in the sciences had already begun to fall significantly. Of this expenditure one million dollars was provided at a 3 per cent interest rate for thirty years. Adding the funds for amortizing the loan brings the total obligation for interest and principle to about $38,000 per year. A matching bank loan to make up the total cost of the building adds another outlay over a five-year period of $131,280. There is also the matter of building upkeep—$96,000, or $84,000 over the expense carried on the old science building. It is obvious that this institution, which may be an extreme though not by any means unique case, has been shackled for a long period by these commitments in the science fields.

Many institutions have incurred similar long-range obligations by borrowing from the government or banks to erect dormitories, student unions, and classroom buildings, and some have encumbered their own endowment funds for similar purposes. As Alter perceptively observes, institutional officers have talked very little in public about the incubus of debt charges they will have to carry for generations of students. Summing up his review of the obligations of institutions of higher education he says: "There are wide variations in the amount of debt and of debt service among institutions. Projection to the total higher educational establishment, however, leads to the conclusion that the total debt may be as high as $8 to $10 billion with an annual debt burden of close to a billion dollars, or a burden of well over $100 per student per year. In some institutions this may run as much as ten times this amount. There are few indeed where the debt burden is zero." [5] Under the conditions which now prevail in the national economy, these recurrent expenditures for plant upkeep require colleges to make crippling diversions of limited resources from essential educational services. In fact, if these continuing budget items could

[5] C. M. Alter, "The Burden of College Debt," *Compact,* October, 1971, 5–5.

be eliminated so might the deficits of some colleges. Since the policies of the federal government largely induced institutions to assume these debts, the Congress might well consider declaring an indefinite moratorium on their payments.

The experience of the past decade vividly suggests, and the fiscal prospects for the seventies imperatively demand that the most frugal criteria be applied to any new building proposals. In fact, institutions should stop all building not absolutely required to maintain their essential services. One building projection which ought to be scrutinized with special care is the library. Its services ought to be determined by the dominant purposes of an undergraduate college and a discriminating assessment of these often will reveal expensive misdirections of effort in library planning. Those colleges, for example, which have stressed the research activities of their faculty members, have added large expenditures for the purchase and storage of thousands of esoteric volumes used only infrequently by a small number of persons. Whether these accessions enhance the institutional image is questionable, and they are a luxury which few colleges can afford. The budgetary items related to the holdings and services of the college library ought to be assessed in terms of real rather than fanciful purposes. To effect substantial savings in buildings, accessions, and services, two or more neighboring institutions, either publicly or privately supported, ought to exhaustively explore all possibilities for combining operations as well as all technological advances in library services.

It is also true that if liberal arts colleges are to discharge their responsibilities of preparing citizens for a full and rich life, their students' esthetic sensitivities must be aroused and cultivated. If the arts are to have their proper place in higher education, even in a time of capital retrenchment colleges will have to find the needed resources. When our society reaches a cultural level at which beauty and esthetic taste are prized as highly as material comfort and well-being, the Congress will pass legislation to redress the imbalance in higher education which has resulted from the appropriation of billions for scientific research and development. Fortunately, our society includes many citizens whose dominant philanthropic interests lie in art and who may be able to fill this cultural gap for the time. These prospective patrons of the arts could doubtless be interested as much in raising the cultural level of future citizens by supporting artistic programs in the colleges as by further enhancing the facilities of galleries, museums, and dramatic enterprises.

As the character and quality of American society change, other demands will arise. Some colleges, but not even a majority, will have to satisfy these social needs. Only prudent and realistic evaluations of these requests by a particular college in terms of the most discriminating use of its limited resources will guarantee that the entire economy and hence the educational value of existing programs will not be impoverished. Computer programs are a case in point. No informed person doubts that computer specialists at all levels will be needed in abundance in the years ahead. It does not follow that every college, or even many of them, should add the related instruction. Yet, at this moment some colleges already in financial difficulty are accepting matching grants for computer facilities and services; eventually the operating costs must be completely offset with institutional funds. Although the total institutional service to society and to individual students may be enhanced by the addition of such programs, these proposals must be appraised in terms of all social needs and particular functions and resources of a given institution.

By uncritically proliferating their services some colleges, in fact, have adulterated not enhanced their total service. Many, especially those of dynamic entrepreneurial impulses, will view any dampening of past expansionist moods as tantamount to stagnation of the entire college enterprise. The alternative policy of using whatever additional resources become available for the enhancement of existing programs deserves more consideration than it has received, however. The future of the liberal arts college will be determined not by the range but rather by the excellence of what it tries to do.

Call To Arms

Any complete analysis of the financial plight of the independent liberal arts colleges drives one to the conclusion that even with maximum success in reducing the costs of operation and gaining added income from private sources, the state and federal governments are the only agencies in our society capable of providing the financial aid which for many will mean the difference between survival or dissolution. As stated earlier, the prospect of adequate support in the immediate financial crisis is not promising. Efforts to persuade representatives in state capitals and in Washington to enact legislation providing various forms of financial help to private institutions have borne fruit at least to the extent of establishing a precedent. Yet, the number of states in which public financial assistance has materially eased the economic plight of colleges is arrestingly small. The likelihood that public assistance will arrive in time to keep the liberal arts colleges afloat is small, unless vigorous political groups are organized in their behalf. If the private colleges have any intention of obtaining public support, they will have to organize more powerful and effective pressure groups at the state and federal levels than now generally exist. If they are to be politically effective these lobby organizations must be manned by persons who from first-hand experience understand the purposes, programs, and potential services of these institutions and who are committed to their preservation. More importantly this staff must possess other traits which are the exception among professional educators: advocates of public support of private colleges must be thoroughly informed and easy participants in the political process as it operates in Washington and the state capitals.

Among the many citizens who are keenly aware of the plight of the colleges are thousands of loyal alumni. In most states the private institutions have not used the influence of their graduates effectively in high government offices. Among the 535 representatives and the 100 senators in Washington and 7,644 legislators in the fifty states, there are many college graduates. Effectively organized, fully briefed, and emotionally motivated prominent alumni could become an irresistible political force, as the graduates of the private colleges of Minnesota showed in the spring of 1971, when they were extremely effective in getting legislation passed which benefitted the private institutions of higher education. If alumni were given a central role in a political action program organized to preserve the quality or perhaps the very existence of their alma mater, they could make the difference between success and failure in the legislatures. Without such a broadly organized and vigorous campaign, the present well-intentioned but middling efforts will be no more effective in the years ahead as they typically have been in the past.

The accomplishment of the necessary reforms will require the unreserved commitment of the entire academic community. The greatest impediment to the improvement of present economic conditions is the divisions that exist among the constituent institutional groups. The various assemblages now loosely described as academic communities are essentially subcultures with widely diversified and often conflicting goals. Recent campus confrontations have thrown into high relief the social separation among boards of trustees, faculties, and student bodies. Less obvious and yet more divisive in any effort to establish generally acceptable institutional goals, are the personal and departmental interests in the academic body itself.

Only a reconstitution of academic government can correct the present lack of organic unity. Few subjects have been so extensively discussed in recent days with so few agreements or constructive results. A principal cause of the fruitlessness of these discourses is their preoccupation with the preservation of the powers, privileges, and perquisites of individuals and groups. Parsons, writing on academic organization, offers this description:

> *This whole set of considerations underlies the fact that the university, with its faculty members as the structural core, has come to be notably loose kind of social organization. The most important things a typical individual member does do not concern the interests of the organization as a whole in any very direct sense. They concern his teaching relations with a small minority of the total student body, the pursuit of his own research interests, which are inevitably in only one of the many fields of knowledge involved in the university, and his active collaboration with a small circle of colleagues. Even the department, at the faculty level, tends to be a highly decentralized body, members of which act corporately only in a very limited sector of their functions, especially those having to do with two matters, namely, their responsibility for a teaching program and the all-important process of recruitment of new members. Except in crisis situations, even all faculty matters, to say nothing of all university matters, are relatively marginal and secondary to the primary professional interests of members.*[6]

A similar disengagement from the general internal policies and practices is characteristic of the board of trustees. Although trustees have legal and moral responsibility for all aspects of institutional life, they have increasingly delegated or,

[6] T. Parsons, "The Strange Case of Academic Organization," *Journal of Higher Education,* June 1971, p. 489.

more accurately, unconsciously relinquished policy-making powers to the faculty and management decisions to the administrators. Except in times of fiscal disarray like the present crisis, the trustees have not concerned themselves with such matters as: the obvious economic consequences of the number of courses and majors offered; the size of faculty teaching loads; the drift of faculty interest to research and outside consultation; the relationship between the overall purposes of the institution and specific needs for new buildings and equipment; the educational merit and the economic impact of various calendar reorganizations; the value to the institution of sabbatical leaves; and the relationship between elitist admission standards and falling enrollments.

Trustees' unconcern about these matters does not spring from any conscious defaulting in their stewardship. On the contrary, trustees generally have believed that by their almost complete delegation of responsibility for academic policy-making they have been acting in the best interest of the institution and of society. This theory of institutional management is now being reconsidered not only by trustees themselves but by the larger company of citizens who must meet the arresting rise in the costs of higher education. Little real improvement can be expected in fiscal management until trustees, at least temporarily, reclaim and exercise many of the responsibilities presently delegated to others.

Where this reversal in institutional policy has already occurred it has brought some charges of invasion of academic freedom. Those who contest the trustees' reassertion of their right to concern themselves about academic policies must be ignorant of the historic meaning of academic freedom—the preservation of the scholar's right to pursue the truth and express it without let or hindrance. Its chief benefactors prostitute the concept when they extend it to include such matters as financial management and curricular contraction. The wisdom of involving the faculty in these latter decisions is now generally recognized and it should be clear that these privileges have nothing to do with academic freedom. Those who confuse the two may lose both.

With regard to faculty members, it must be said at once that if they have not been as fully responsible in controlling the rising costs of higher education as could be wished, they have rarely been brought into the related discussions. In the game of fiscal management trustees and administrators have typically played their cards close to the chest. Hence, faculties have had neither the requisite knowledge nor the motivation to restrain expenditures. Unless they become full participants in the revision of policies and practices designed to reduce operating expenses, institutional life will remain devitalized and to some extent misdirected.

Sound argument can also be made for student participation in decision-making. They or their parents pay the bills, their lives are beneficially or adversely affected by the character and quality of their education. On some matters they are less well informed than trustees or faculties; on others, they are better informed and more objective. This generation of students is strikingly more concerned than their predecessors about the ends of higher education. As a practical matter, colleges eager to attract more students ought to recognize that they will gravitate to those institutions where they are given roles in the policy-making process. (The subject is discussed at length in *Should Students Share the Power?,* by Temple University Press.)

Institutions which wish to effect economies sufficient to assure their survival ought to so reconstruct their deliberative and legislative machinery as to embrace all constituent groups. Complete information related to matters at issue ought to be laid before these bodies without reservation so that the purpose, the necessity, and the equity of contemplated economies will be understood and accepted with good will. If the necessary savings are to be realized without long-range damage all members of the academic community must feel that they are making their own contribution to the preservation of the institution with which they have cast their lot. In the absence of such an inclusive commitment, all inside as well as outside efforts to regain lasting financial health while maintaining educational integrity will fail.

Academic people as a group have been known for their social consciousness and dedication to the common good. They may be expected again to respond favorably to any proposal which involves them in the revision of policies and practices essential to the preservation of the institutions that consistently have served this country with distinction. The history of the liberal arts colleges is replete with examples of selfless dedication to enterprises that have encountered severe financial problems. The problems today are somewhat different and require different solutions, but the indispensable ingredients in the cure for the financial malady are wisdom in planning, boldness in execution, and unswerving commitment. There is an abundance of these qualities among the members of the college communities. If they can be mustered in a unified attack on today's problems, the colleges will not only survive but continue their unique contribution to the well-being of our society.

Index

A

Academic culture: changing, 43–49; described, 43–44; liberation from, 45–49
Academic freedom related to trustees and academic policies, 149–150
Academic government, reconstitution of, 147–151
Accountability and instructional technology, 9, 84, 96–97, 98
Adaptation: in composition course, 94; in instructional technology, 91–92, 94, 97
Administration: and institutional purposes, 134; trustees' role in, 148–149
Admissions: deferred, 109; inadequate criteria for, 136–137; nontraditional grades related to graduate school, 75
Advancement placement, 26
Air Training Center, productivity through programed instruction at, 96
ALTER, C. M., 143
Alumni: donations of, 130; as lobbyists for government aid, 147
Antioch College: course credit records at, 67; as intellectual-expressive institution, 68; project-oriented studies at, 8, 78–84, 103, 110, 112; student response to nongrading at, 74–76; Washington-Baltimore Campus of, 78–84
Architecture and learning environment, 104–105
Arts in higher education, 144–145
Attitude change, necessary, 5, 11
Authoritarianism and learning productivity, 69
Autonomy in human development, 18–20

B

BAKAN, D., 8, 70–78
BARRETT, L., 110
Behavioral objectives. *See* Operational objectives
Berea College, significant learning spaces at, 110
BLOOM, M., 35–43
BOGART, H., 113
BOWEN, H. R., 70
BOYER, E., 107–108

C

Cambridge University, government intrusion in, 131
CASSIDY, S. W., 7–8, 50–61
Changes, utility of, 63–64
Chicago, University of: student in-group at, 57; student self-education at, 55–56
CHICKERING, A. W., 7, 11, 13–29, 78, 84
Class size and unit costs, 138–139
Colegio Jacinto Trevino, 79, 81–82
College community: commitment to reform of, 147–151; as responsible for setting purposes, 134
Colleges: commitment to reform by, 146–151; course proliferation in, 135–136; fiscal problems of small, 127–151; proliferation of services at, 145–146; student movement away from, 102–114. *See also* Liberal arts colleges
Communes as off-campus learning environments, 105–106
Community colleges, transfer students from, 139–140
Community service, increased programs of, 27
Competence: community talent used to enlarge faculty, 83; linked to freedom and work, 71–72, 77; role in human development of, 17–20, 84; as stage in faculty development, 37–40
Composition course as systems model, 94–96
Computer programs and proliferation of services, 145
Consciousness: change in faculty, 7, 48; students' new, 33–34, 36
Continuing education, 24
Contracted studies: compared with Bakan Plan, 70–78; at Evergreen State College, 8, 64–69; rationale for, 64–65
Cooperative plan: and graduate school admission, 75; student response to, 104
Coordinated studies compared with contracted studies, 64–65
Corporations and college management, 129–130
Costs, educational: of Bakan Plan, 70; and instructional technology, 96; related to productivity, 28; and tutorials, 73; unit, 11, 138–139
Courses: proliferation of, 135–136; record of credit for,

Courses (Cont.)
67, 70, 74–75
Curriculum: educational technology and joint faculty-student investigation in, 110–114; individualized instruction in, 25–26

D

Danforth Workshop for Liberal Education, 64, 68, 71
DE LISLE, F. H., 25–27
Decision process of students in choosing a college, 123–126
Decoy, Kentucky, learning environment at, 99–102, 108, 114
Discipline, academic: faculty identification with, 7, 43; influence on liberal education of, 5; student choice of, 53
Discovery, importance to students of, 53
DOERMANN, H., 120–121, 129
Donors, role of in college finances, 128–130
DOUGLASS, G. K., 70
DRESSEL, P. L., 25–27
DRUCKER, P., 22–23, 86–87
DUFF, F., 100, 114
DUFF, L., 100, 114

E

Education: continuing, 24; costs of, 11, 28, 70, 73, 96, 138–139; expenditures for, 21; impeded, unresponsive, and outmoded, 87–88; implication of social change and human development for, 21–29; improvement of through instructional technology, 89–93; integrated with experience, 22, 27, 74, 78–84, 102–105; principles of new forms of, 22; purposes of, 28–29, 133–134; reform of through freedoms to teach and learn, 70–71; timing and intensity of, 22–24; universal, 117–118
Enrollment, noncontinuous, 109
Entering behavior: in composition course, 94; in instructional technology model, 90–91
ERIKSON, E., 38
Evaluative feedback, 76–78
Evergreen State College: contracted studies program at, 8, 64–69; faculty competence at, 71–72; and separated curriculum, 110; study and action programs at, 78
Expectations, student-faculty agreement on, 69
External degrees, 107–108

F

Facilities, debt burdens for, 141–144
Faculty: and academic government, 148, 150; changing function of, 7; development of, 37–40, 48–49; identification with disciplines by, 7, 43; and improvement of instruction,

Faculty (Cont.)
93; and institutional purposes, 134; integration-of-values response by, 35, 41–43; intellectual, 58; as isolated or social children, 37–38; meaningful influence of, 54–55, 57, 59; as models for students, 52–53, 58; patterns of response to new student behavior of, 7, 35–43, 66; radical-accommodation response of, 35, 40–41; related to student cultures, 8; response to new values of, 30–49; rewards for, 44, 72, 135; role of in contracted studies, 65–69; role of in instructional technology, 96; Socratic, 58–59, 60–61, 109; standpat response of, 35, 36–37, 38–39; and student self-education, 50–61; university influence on, 4

Feedback, evaluative, student need for, 76–78

Fieldwork programs, increase in, 27

Fiscal problems of liberal arts colleges, 127–151

Foundations, role in college finance of, 130

Four-one-four calendar, joint investigations in, 112

FREEDMAN, M., 33

Freedom: academic, 149–150; of teachers and students in Bakan Plan, 9, 70–71, 77

Freshman year, meaningful professor in, 54–56, 59

Friends University, student response to co-op program at, 104

GIOVANNI, 11–12

Goals: faculty-student agreement on, 8, 69; in liberating faculty from academic culture, 45; renewal of, 11

GOLDSMITH, J., 35–36

Government aid to private colleges: necessity of, 146–147; trustee reluctance to accept, 131–132

Grades, absence of in Bakan Plan, 74–76

Graduate study, impact of nongrading on plans for, 75

Great Britain: Open University in, 107–108; University Grants Committee in, 131

Guidelines for program design, 8, 68–69

H

High School Equivalency Program of Colegio Jacinto Trevino, 79, 81–82

HILBERRY, C., 9–10, 99–114

HOLLAND, J. L., 136–137

HOLLISTER, B., 62–63

Honors programs, 26

Housing, college, variety in, 109

Human development, 7; and individual instruction, 26; major areas of, 17–21

Human relations in industry and education, 31

I

Incorporation of institutional functioning as part of student self-education, 52, 56

Independent study: in Bakan Plan, 71; as individualized instruction, 26; programed methods with teacher-objectives for, 83; student responsibility for, 8, 50–61

Individualized instruction: in integration of experience and education, 24–27; and instructional technology, 97; need for, 120; related to Keeton's principles, 83

Institutions: functioning of, 52, 56; humanizing of, 47–48

Instructional technology, 9; Commission on, 87–88, 92–93, 96; and educational improvement, 89–93; and the liberal arts college, 97–98; model of, 89–92; and off-campus learning environments, 107–108, 111; related to Keeton's principles, 83; results of utilizing, 94–97; rewards of, 86–98

Integration of education and experience: in Bakan Plan, 74; and individualized instruction, 27; in learning environments, 102–105; as principle of learning, 22; in project-oriented studies, 78–84

Integrity in human development, 19–20, 84

Interdisciplinary study: in Antioch seminars, 72; in Evergreen's contracted studies, 65, 71–72; in project-oriented studies, 81–82

Interim terms, 26

J

Joint student-faculty investigations in separated curriculum, 9, 112–114

Junior colleges, enrollment history of, 139

K

Kalamazoo College: classroom environment at, 104; and off-campus learning, 103

KEETON, M. T., 8–9, 62–85, 112

KELLER, G., 107–108

L

Learning: authoritarianism and, 69; environments for, 10, 99–114; improvement of through instructional technology, 95, 97; integration of affective, value-based, and cognitive, 4, 7; in learning modules and joint investigations, 110–114; media for, 26, 119–120; modules for, 9, 111–112, 114; off-campus, 102–114; paths for, 91; self-

Learning (Cont.)
amplifying effect of, 23; student-faculty agreement on types of, 69
LEWIN, K., 38
Liberal arts colleges: aims of, 2–7; fiscal problems of, 127–151; independence and intent of, 133–146; and instructional technology, 97–98; issues and options of, 2–7; in the mass market, 118–120; reform of, 70–71, 146–151. *See also* Colleges
Liberal education: alternative pathways in, 62–85; design principles for, 68–69, 77–78, 82; priorities in, 84–85
Library, services and savings of, 144
Loans to colleges, consequences of, 141–143
Lobbying, for government aid to private colleges, 146–147
LUTZ, S. W., 137n

M

MC CLEERY, M., 62–63
MC GRATH, E. J., 10–11, 127–151
Management, 11; mechanical theory of, 30; need for in liberal arts colleges, 132–133; organic, 31; role of trustees and administration in, 148–149
Marketing of higher education, 10; analysis in, 115–126; role of mass market in, 119; variables in, 116–117
Measurable objectives. *See* Operational objectives
Media: for individualized instruction, 26, 92; standardized instructional, 119–120
MENDELSOHN, H., 10, 115–126
MEYER, G., 55–56
Middle Patuxent Valley Natural Inventory, 79–81
Minnesota community colleges, transfer plans of students in, 140
Modules, learning, 9, 111–112, 114
Monteith College: meaningful professor at, 54–55; student cultures at, 56–58; student-organized curriculum at, 51; student-teacher relationship at, 60–61
Motivation: in instructional technology, 92; as learning support, 8, 69, 77
Multimedia learning center, 9

N

New York State Education Department, external degrees of, 108
NICOSIA, F., 124–126
Nongrading in Bakan Plan, 74–76
NORTH, S. R., 9, 83, 84, 86–98, 107, 111

O

Objectives. *See* Operational objectives
Off-campus study, impetus toward, 102–114

Oklahoma Christian College, freshman composition course on systems model at, 94–96
Open University, 107–108
Operational objectives: in composition course, 94; in educational productivity, 6, 9; in instructional technology, 89–90, 92, 96–97; and learning environments, 107, 111; set by college community, 11
Oxford University, 131

P

PARSONS, T., 148
Permanent records. *See* Transcripts
Philanthropists: and the arts in higher education, 145; role of in college financing, 129
Policy-making powers of faculty and trustees, 148–149
POSTLETHWAIT, S. N., 95
Private colleges in the mass market, 118–120. *See also* Liberal arts colleges
Problem solving as aim of liberal education, 2–3
Productivity, educational, 1; defined, 5–7; improved through instructional technology, 9, 95–97
Proficiency exams in Bakan Plan, 74
Programed instruction, 11; productivity increases as result of, 96. *See also* Instructional technology
Programs, design principles for liberal arts, 8, 68–69
Project-oriented studies, 8; at Antioch's Washington-Baltimore Campus, 78–84
Purposes: of education, 28–29; in human development, 17–20; institutional, 133–134

R

RALPH, N., 35–43
Reed College: "beat" subculture in, 36; cultural polarization and tuition boycott at, 35–36; as intellectual-expressive institution, 68
Reference groups: faculty identification with, 7; students as, 40
Reform of liberal arts colleges: commitment to, 146–151; through freedoms to teach and learn, 70–71
Residence halls, increased education in, 27
Resource allocations, 11, 138–146
Response patterns: identified, 35; origin of, 37–43
RICHARDS, J. M., JR., 137n
Rosewood State Training School Videotape, 79, 81

S

Sabbatical leave plan, 61
San Francisco Bay Area, faculty response to new values in, 33–35
San Francisco State College, new student consciousness at, 33

SANFORD, N., 7, 11, 30–49, 66, 69, 109
Sciences, building proliferation and enrollment decline in, 141–143
SCOTT, J. H. M., 131n
Self-development: of liberal arts college students, 2–7; as prime motivation, 16, 20–21, 29
Self-discovery stage in faculty development, 38, 40, 43
Self-expansion as prime motivation, 16, 20–21, 29
Self-renewal, education for, 4–6
Self-study in faculty development, 47
Seminars: as individualized instruction, 26; as joint student-faculty investigation, 113–114; paradoxes of, 66–67; in project-oriented studies, 81–82
Social change: and higher education, 7, 14–16, 18; in individualized instruction, 26
Social trends, information on needed, 10, 122–123
Space, environmental, 109–110
Stanford University, new student consciousness at, 33
State University of New York, external degrees of, 107–108
STERN, G. G., 68
STINE, R. D., 1–12
Structural change to improve campus learning environment, 108–114; noncontinuous enrollment as, 109; expansion of learning spaces as, 109–110; separated curriculum as, 110–114
Student-teacher relationship: in Bakan Plan, 70–71; importance of, 59–61; in separated curriculum, 110–114; time for, 43–44
Students: as consumers of higher education, 117–126; evaluation of in systems model, 91–92; faculty identification with, 7; faculty time with, 43–44; and institutional purposes, 134; intellectually and financially qualified, 120–121; new consciousness of, 33–34, 36; noncontinuous enrollment by, 109; participation in academic government by, 150; participation in education by, 52–56; preferences for unique colleges of, 121–122; response to cooperative programs of, 104; response to nongrading of, 74–76; responsibility for own education of, 8, 50–61, 93; six cultures among, 8, 56–60; typologies of, 10
Systems approach to educational improvement, 9, 89–93
Systems evaluation in instructional technology, 92

T

Teaching, improvement of: Bakan Plan for, 71; in-

Teaching (Cont.)
hibited by academic culture, 7, 45–49
Terminal behavior in instructional technology model, 89–90
THOMPSON, M. M., 26
TICKTON, S. G., 87–88, 93n
Timing and intensity of education, 22–24
Transcripts: of courses and credits at Antioch, 67; of courses in Bakan Plan, 70, 74
Transfer students from community colleges, 138–140
Trustees: and academic freedom, 149; and academic government, 148–150; and government aid to private colleges, 131–132; and institutional purposes, 134
Tuition: boycott of at Reed College, 35–36; diminishing returns in rise of, 128–129
Tutorials: in Bakan Plan, 70, 72–73; in composition course, 94; as individualized instruction, 26; paradoxes of, 66–67
TWYFORD, L. C., JR., 95n

U

Understanding of others and self, 18–20, 84
Unitarian Seminary, new student consciousness at, 33–34
Unit costs: need to decrease, 11; for upper- and lower-classmen, 138–139
University Grants Committee, impact on Oxford and Cambridge of, 131
University of California, Berkeley, new values at, 32

V

Values, faculty response to new student, 30–49
Vassar College, student protest at, 30–31

W

Washington. *See* Evergreen State College
Wayne State University. *See* Monteith College
Wilberforce University, student response to co-op program at, 104
WILLIAMS, W. C., 57
WERTHMAN, C., 55–56
Work loads, faculty, linked to freedom and competence, 71–73, 77
Work roles and educational roles, 30–32
Work-study programs, 75, 104
Wright Institute, interviews on faculty response to new values by, 35–47